Lethal
Justice

Lethal Justice

One Man's Journey of Hope on Death Row

Joy Elder

New City

Published in Great Britain and the United States of America by
New City, 57 Twyford Ave., London, W3 9PZ and
New City Press, 202 Cardinal Rd., Hyde Park, NY 12538
Copyright © 2002 by Joy Elder

Scripture quotations are taken from *The Jerusalem Bible*.
Copyright © 1966, 1967 and 1968 by Darton, Longman & Todd
and Doubleday & Company, Inc.

Cover design by Nick Cianfarani

ISBN (British ed.): 0-904287-80-7
ISBN (U.S. ed.): 1-56548-164-X

Library of Congress Cataloging-in-Publication Data:

Elder, Joy.
    Lethal Justice : one man's journey of hope on death row / Joy Elder.
        p. cm.
    ISBN 1-56548-164-X
        1. Gosch, Lesley, d. 1998. 2. Death row inmates--Texas--Biography. 3. Death row
    inmates--Texas--Correspondence. I. Title.

HV9475.T7 E56 2001
364.15'23'092--dc21   2001051193

Printed in Canada

To Lesley . . .
and all who still languish on death row
in Huntsville, Texas

Oftentimes have I heard you speak of one who commits a wrong as though he were not one of you, but a stranger unto you and an intruder upon your world.

But I say that even as the holy and the righteous cannot rise beyond the highest which is in each and every one of you,

So the wicked and the weak cannot fall lower than the lowest which is in you also.

And as a single leaf turns not yellow but with the silent knowledge of the whole tree,

So the wrong-doer cannot wrong without the hidden will of you all.

Like a procession you walk together towards your god-self.

You are the way and the wayfarers.

And when one of you falls down he falls for those behind him, a caution against the stumbling stone.

Ay, and he falls for those ahead of him, who, though faster and surer of foot, yet removed not the stumbling stone.

Kahlil Gibran, *The Prophet*

Contents

Lesley

A short man, forty-two years old, with thick black spectacles, is being prepared for death by lethal injection.

He is dressed completely in white and is made to lie down on a bed of white.

His arms are stretched out in the form of a cross.

He is bound from head to foot and at his wrists.

His eyes are tightly shut.

He makes no sound.

His stomach falls and rises.

It stops doing so.

Lesley Gosch lies dead.

Rebecca

The wife of Frank Patton, bank president, lies slumped in a pool of blood in her own home.

She has six gunshot wounds to her head.

Her husband and his daughter, Amy, age fifteen, are inconsolable.

Who could have done this dreadful deed?

Joy

A nun from North Wales looks on as Lesley receives three fatal injections: one to relax the muscles, one to stop the breathing, and one to arrest the heart.

She and five other of his friends are led away from the killing room.

Now they are in front of the last electronically-controlled door.

They walk outside.

The sun is warm and the birds are singing.

In front of them is a neat garden of roses.

Margôt

Joy's friend from North Wales keeps vigil outside the prison walls.

With a handful of other protestors she holds a banner which reads: "WALES AGAINST THE DEATH PENALTY."

They all stand in silence, praying and grieving that yet another life is being taken.

Introduction

Some years ago I happened to flick onto the second showing of a BBC film called *Fourteen Days in May*. It was about the final fourteen days of a very personable young black man, Edward Earl Johnson, about to be executed in Mississippi. A British film crew went out to record the last days of his life. A young dedicated British lawyer, Clive Stafford-Smith, had been brought in to act in his defense, but it was too late to save Edward. He went to his death in the gas chamber after a moving prayer service and gentle hymn singing with his family. After his death, his innocence was proved.

As a result of the first showing of this film in 1987, people began writing to some prisoners on death row, and an organization was formed for the sole purpose of putting people in the U. K. in touch with death row prisoners. It grew and eventually a second one called "Human Writes" evolved. Every single letter-writer is a window to the world and a lifeline of hope to prisoners awaiting execution.

About six months after seeing that film, I responded to an invitation to join Human Writes and was given the name of Lesley Gosch in Texas. It was August 1997 when things really started to move. They have been moving ever since.

The crime for which Lesley was convicted involved the fatal shooting of the wife of Frank Patton, President of Castle Hills National Bank, San Antonio, Texas. Events took place as follows:

18 September 1985

An unknown male had instructed Mr. Patton to gather cash together in a briefcase and to go directly to the payphones at the food area at the North Star Mall in San Antonio. The caller told Mr. Patton that he had precisely forty-five minutes to comply with these directions or his wife would be killed.

After hanging up the phone, Mr. Patton directed a bank cashier to begin gathering the money together, while his secretary called the FBI. Seven minutes after the initial extortion call, officers from the Alamo Heights Police Department arrived at the Pattons' home to find Rebecca Patton lying dead on the floor.

23 September 1985

San Antonio bankers offered a one hundred thousand-dollar reward leading to the arrest, indictment and conviction of the person responsible for the murder.

25 September 1985

JR and Lesley Gosch are named as those responsible, by a third person who claimed the reward.

14 August 1986

JR alleged that Lesley Gosch was the one who entered the Patton house and shot Mrs. Patton.

26 August 1986

The guilt-innocence phase of Lesley Gosch's trial began in Victoria, Texas. The state's evidence was largely circumstantial. The *only* direct evidence that Lesley Gosch was the person who shot Mrs. Patton was that of JR, who had an obvious motive to transfer responsibility to Lesley Gosch in order to deflect suspicion from himself.

2 September 1986

Lesley Gosch was sentenced to die.

The San Antonio Express News (29 September 1985) reported as follows: "Mr. Patton appears to be a courageous and resilient individual who derives much of his strength from his Christian faith. Shortly after the sentencing he publicly stated that 'life in prison [for his wife's killers], with no chance of parole, would be adequate punishment in my view.' "

Mr. Patton himself wrote: "During this time I suffered an awesome sense of emptiness, but I also became aware of a spiritual consciousness that was not my own. God filled this emptiness in my heart with his love before it would be filled with hate. That is why I could do nothing but forgive the killer and express no hatred." And: "My hope and prayer would be that these men come to know Jesus Christ and be forgiven and have their lives changed

. . . who knows? Some day we may all be in heaven together."

When I received my first letter from Lesley, I was astounded at the style of the letter itself and at his extraordinary signature.

This letter, and the many that followed, were almost stark in their simplicity and directness; Lesley didn't "waste" a single word or thought. He had the rare ability to capture the most profound thoughts in the shortest possible way. He didn't speak much about his feelings, which at first was a little bit disappointing. But gradually I came to find, know, and love this person who, as a child, had been diagnosed as autistic. I don't actually think he was autistic, but the autistic-like behavior he displayed was his way of coping with a very traumatic childhood.

Lesley always had the seeds of a gentle, brilliant, and caring person. Unfortunately, abuse, isolation, and cruelty combined with Lesley's innate personality to compel a complete withdrawal from people in general, and to render him susceptible to other, more powerful forces—both those of his step grandfather and a friend, JR He was drawn into a world of crime fashioned by JR, who exacted revenge on Lesley by setting him up for the murder of Mrs. Patton in exchange for statements given by Lesley ten years earlier implicating JR in aggravated robbery.

Lesley came into the world an unwanted child. His mother Rose was just sixteen, and his father Ronald Tontz was seventeen. Rose and Ronald married, but it was just a "spur of the moment" affair. Ronald is remembered in family anecdotes and photographs as a teenage James Dean—handsome and intelligent, but restless and bored with school, preferring to spend his time drinking, carousing and racing "hot rods." Rose had a very hard upbringing in which she had been forced into working in her family's dry-cleaning business at weekends and after school. Ronald's carefree and rather reckless lifestyle had a refreshing appeal for her, and soon these two young people began to date. They then moved to Kansas. Soon after this Ronald Tontz was killed in a car crash.

Once in Kansas, Rose fell into a deep depression that worsened after she gave birth to Lesley, and soon the young couple no longer even pretended to care for Lesley. When Ronald's mother, Eva, wanted to adopt him, they gladly relinquished him; and, once Eva and her second husband Wesley Gosch had signed the adoption papers, Rose and Ronald had no further involvement in the upbringing of their son.

Yet despite his early history, which was turbulent in the extreme, Lesley is remembered by family members as an exceptionally gentle child.

Lesley's step grandfather, Wesley Gosch, was a master gunsmith. He was determined to introduce Lesley to guns while he was still a child, but when the five-year-old was given a rifle he ignored it and played with his other toys. Several years later, Wesley forced Lesley to shoot a deer. This upset him greatly. He told an aunt that he was disgusted by his step grandfather's insistence that he kill it, but he felt he had no choice because of the threats of severe beatings.

Eventually Eva got cancer and died when Lesley was ten years old. She had desperately wanted her sister to take Lesley and care for him, but Wesley Gosch was opposed to it. Wesley was, according to reports contained in documents, a "sadistic, tyrannical braggart who sought to dominate and control those around him in order to prop up his own inflated ego." He had abused

Lesley from an early age, and now Lesley had lost the loving protection of his grandmother. He was routinely beaten by Wesley, and a long, dark period in Lesley's life followed. Wesley isolated him from other children and from other family members, and so gradually Lesley began to withdraw into a lonely, autistic, fantasy world. The torment of his inner life can only be imagined.

Yet somehow Lesley managed to develop intellectually and spiritually in the midst of this abuse, isolation and unreality. In 1969 he received the Eagle Scout award after his long-time involvement in scouting.

From an early age Lesley had been very interested in science, and he continued to grow in his knowledge of physics. Eventually he enrolled at the University of Texas, San Antonio. However, his social inexperience and inability to deal with the world left him open to manipulation. His old school friend, JR, taller and almost double Lesley's size, dragged Lesley into the robbery of two pharmacies during which JR almost killed a pharmacist. Lesley restrained him just in time. JR was given a ten-year sentence—Lesley was commended for saving the pharmacist's life and put on probation.

Around this time, Lesley was trying to escape from his step grandfather's control, setting up an independent household with a Mexican girlfriend, Georgina Morejon, to whom he was later married for five years until she was tragically killed in a car crash in May 1986. Like Lesley's father in his youth, Georgina had loved living life in the fast lane.

1

Lesley's Letters,
1992–1997

From the time of his incarceration, Lesley blossomed. Ironically, like so many others on death row, he finally found routine and stability in his life, dreadful though life on death row is. He became an extremely talented artist and craftsman, producing pen and ink drawings and oil paintings that are stunning in their detail and accuracy. Registered blind, Lesley had to do all his artwork with his face almost one inch from the paper. This required an infinite amount of patience and skill. The flutes he made were copied from those created by the early American Indians.

He also made an accurate recreation of a Viking ship, painstakingly reproduced—even down to the exact number of movable oars.

He spoke five languages and read voraciously.

Apart from his talents, Lesley used much of his time reaching out to and helping others, both on death row and outside. For a while he began a jewelry "business," paying others on the row to make earrings and necklaces to sell in the free world. He used the profits to compile "welcome" bags for the newly arriving inmates. These bags would include articles such as toothpaste, combs and other small items. Using his sharp intellect, he helped other inmates to understand the legal morass through which their cases were proceeding, and assisted them in drafting legal motions or letters to attorneys.

It was 1992 when I first began writing to Lesley, my first death row friend. He wasn't the easiest person to get to know. His letters, while friendly, were rather formal and cerebral, but very profound. Lesley rarely "poured his heart out." His thoughts were always expressed succinctly and you had to read between the lines to tap into his carefully protected emotional life. I soon realized that he was a highly intelligent, well-educated person. Much later on I was told that he was a genius, which I can well believe. I had no idea at all what he looked like. I knew that he worked in the prison garment factory and I would imagine him sitting at his machine: a tall thin man with thin glasses and a thin smile. I couldn't have been more wrong!

One thread that ran through almost all of his letters was some news about his on-going legal work which consumed a vast amount of his time as he had to do most of it himself. In the beginning he had a lawyer who was so useless that he had to let him go. It wasn't until the last three years before his execution that he finally got two excellent ones, Raoul Schonemann and Maurie Levin, who did all in their power to save him.

On 6 September 1993 Lesley had written to me:

Dear Joy:

Please forgive me for not answering your previous letters but this has been a terrible year for me. Things started downhill last January, when I was forced to fire my attorney because he wasn't conducting my appeal as he had agreed to when I hired him. This was a very difficult decision as it effectively made me my own lawyer. Then in May, after waiting over five years for their decision, the appeal court ruled against me. This move put me in line to receive an execution date, which occurred during the second week of July. I was taken from the prison back to my home town of San Antonio, approximately 350 miles away. There, a formal hearing was held in the court in which I was tried some eight years ago. At this hearing, the judge issued my death warrant: to be executed on the morning of September 17th, 1993. This is what a "bench warrant" is all about. It is the legal document ordering my return for the hearing.

Lesley went on to explain what happens when a prisoner is bench-warranted:

When we are transported away from the prison for short periods, I was only gone for 8 days, we are not permitted to take our property along with us. I guess they feel that the facility we are going to can handle our needs during our stay. Naturally, while

I was away some of my property was "lost" by the prison. This is one of their standard intimidation procedures, the threat of loss or damage to your personal possessions.

At the time of receiving that letter, I was caring for my elderly father in the final stages of his life. Lesley had expressed his concern:

I am sorry to hear about the "situation" with your father. After going through pretty much the same thing with my own father about 10 years ago I can relate to how you feel. He is greatly blessed to have a daughter who will care for him. Many fathers don't.

He closed his letter:

Take good care of yourself (and thereby those who depend on you) and write again soon. I'll be here!

I wondered what his "father" would have been like and tried to imagine Lesley caring for him. It was only later on that I would finally get a much fuller picture of Lesley's life story. Up until that time, I believe most of it was too painful for him to share.

Soon after receiving that letter, my father's condition deteriorated. I had initially returned to Wales to care for my mother who was ill with cancer. It had been a hard move to make as it had meant leaving behind many people I loved and an entire way of life in Liverpool. I had been blessed with wonderful parents who had never put any obstacles in my way as I followed the vocation that took me to Africa and beyond. Therefore in *their* hour of need I had known exactly what I had to do. It was very similar to how I would later feel when receiving Lesley's invitation to visit Texas. Those were two moments in my life when I "just knew" what had to be done. Both were hugely significant decisions.

I would try to imagine the prison, and Lesley sitting in his eight-by-five-foot cell. Sitting writing. Drawing. Painting. Meditating. Making flutes.

Not only did Lesley write to me, he also wrote to some of the young people I worked with in my local parish of Saint Joseph's. He was brilliant with them, knowing exactly how to respond to their particular interests.

He wrote to Amy, aged thirteen, on 15 October 1993:

Dear Amy:

Thank you very much for your letter of September the 28th. I am sorry for not writing sooner but lately most of my time is being spent helping my attorney work on my appeal. This is no fun, but absolutely necessary. I am quite impressed with your printing. Being an engineer before I came to prison, I did a great deal of it, drawing up plans and schedules. Most folks don't know how much practice is required to develop clear lettering. I'm slow, so I cheat and use a typewriter. I was born on July 8th, 1955. Yes, I know that was a long time ago, it feels like it too! By the way, happy birthday to you. How does it feel to be a "teenager" now? You write in your letter that you once had a bydji. What's a bydji, some form of peculiar animal from the South Pacific? Do they have a Buddha-nature? I also read in

your letter that you go dancing every
Wednesday? Is this a formal dance class
which you attend, perhaps with your sister
Helen? It's good to have a hobby like that, I
draw and paint myself. Not literally, I
paint pictures. I like doing pictures of
animals, particularly the big cats (lions,
tigers, leopards, and the like). This also
provides me with a good income so I can
afford to paint. It's amazing how expensive
art supplies have gotten. But I think I would
paint even if I got nothing for my work. For
me, it's like getting paid to eat ice cream.
I think that everyone's work should be like
that. What sort of topics do you talk about
in school? Which ones do you like to talk
about? I see that you like to read. So do I.
What type of books do you like best? I read a
lot of comparative religion and philosophy.
Well, thank you for thinking about and
praying for me. Prayer is the greatest gift
that you can give anyone, for it brings to
their aid the very power which created the
universe! Take care of yourself and write
again soon.

(Bydji was in fact meant to be *budgie!*—a small Australian parakeet.)

And to Gareth, also aged thirteen, on 7 November
1993:

Dear Gareth:

Thank you very much for your letter of September the 28th. I'm sorry for not getting back to you sooner but things have been a bit chaotic here for the past few weeks and I haven't been able to. So how is life treating you? Well, I hope! Things here on death row are not quite as bad as you might imagine. For example, rather than being forced to stay in a cell all day, we are allowed to work if we want. I work four hours a day in a garment factory running a sewing machine. The part of the factory I work in produces uniform pants for the prison guards. This arrangement may sound a little strange, but life in prison is a bit weird anyway, so it fits in perfectly. We don't get paid for our work as in a "normal" garment factory. Instead the prison officials allow us additional forms of recreation. For example, I like to draw and paint. So as a reward for my work, I am allowed to purchase certain approved art supplies. I don't want this to sound like I'm only allowed to buy a few pencils and some paper. I can get paint, brushes, canvas, you name it! Right now, I'm working on a painting of a Siberian tiger. What do you do for entertainment? I read in your letter that you are learning a new play. Which role have you been assigned? The way my luck runs, I'd end up playing the snake. In any event, good luck with the play to all of you. Well, I think

```
that I'll close this letter with a riddle.
And the riddle is: What one thing is there,
that once known, everything knowable is
known? Let me know what you think the answer
is. In the meantime, take good care of your-
self.
```

It was typical of Lesley's sensitivity that he had kept a light-hearted touch, not wishing to depress the children by exposing them to the darker side of life on "the row." His love of art, religion and study were, however, actually transforming his life. Through his spiritual and intellectual activity he was able to transcend the horrors of his environment.

On 8 December 1993 he wrote:

```
Dear Joy:
Many thanks to you and your kids for the
numerous cards and letters. They have
brought a bit of sunshine into a twilight
world. I'm sorry that I haven't always been
able to respond in a timely manner, but my
appeal is presently in an "active" phase and
the pleadings require almost constant
attention. I spent the last three weeks of
November on yet another bench warrant—to
receive a new execution date: April the
15th. My attorneys tell me that I have abso-
lutely nothing to worry about, and are
correct, but not for the reasons they think.
God gives us exactly what we need, precisely
when we need it most—so what is there to
worry about?
```

One of the many things which I have been meaning to do but just haven't had the time, is to collect several examples of my artwork and send them to you and your kids. Perhaps this card will be a first step toward that goal. Several years ago, the staff of the HOPE anti-death penalty organization contacted me and asked that I donate some of my artwork to help in one of their fund raisers. It was almost Christmas, so I did something to fit the season, a technical pen drawing of a Canadian Lynx kitten playing with a Christmas ornament. One thing led to another and the drawing got turned into the Christmas card you're now holding. By the way, this is my <u>first</u> pen and ink drawing. I'm presently working on a fantasy pen and ink which will be reproduced as a poster and sold to raise money so that the families of those on death row who cannot normally afford the travel expenses of a visit will be able to come for a Christmas visit.

Well, I had better close as I'm running out of both time and space. You all take care and remember God, because He never forgets us.

Sincerely;
Lesley Gosch

P.S.: Is life, like a moving song, any less beautiful because it has an end?

Merry Christmas!

I stared and stared at the postscript of this letter, knowing that his life really could be cut short one day. I found it just so poignant. There he was, waiting to be killed and he was concentrating on artwork that would raise funds to help others.

It was in December 1997, four years later, that I had the Canadian lynx kitten made into a Christmas card of my own. All who received it were moved by it, and it is now framed and hanging on my wall.

Between December 1993 and January 1995 there was a total gap in our writing. I think it was due to pressures at both ends: Lesley was working frantically on his appeals and I was coping with my father's last illness, death and the aftermath of it. The last communication in 1993 was a short letter and a piece of his literary work:

Dear Joy:

Thank you very much for your letter of December the 5th and the copy of The Wing of Friendship. I can only applaud you and your kids' ingenuity in putting the Lord's teachings into practice. For did He not say that His disciples would be known by their actions?

Things in my case have taken an unexpected turn for the worse. The federal judge who granted my stay of execution has withdrawn it because he has decided that my case does not fall within his jurisdiction. So during the last week of November, I was again returned to San Antonio and given a new execution date: April the 15th. My attorneys assure me that this date will be stayed as well because there are many issues yet to be resolved in my case. Only time will tell though.

As I may have written you earlier, I do short magazine articles as a second source of income. A news reporter who has read some of my work recently did an interview, during which she asked: "How do you feel about being cursed to spend perhaps your last days on death row?" When I told her that being on death row was not a curse, but a blessing, her jaw hit the floor. And to explain my position, I gave her a copy of the little story I have included here. Merry Christmas!

MY SERVANT, MY FORTUNE
as retold by
Lesley L. Gosch

In the city of Jerusalem in ancient Israel there lived a wealthy merchant. His house was decked with ornaments and precious furnishings, and was designed by the most talented architects of the day. His visitors and clientele were of the highest class and were accustomed to only the best treatment and the most lavish entertainment that high society could afford.

One day the merchant hired a new servant. And it soon became apparent that the man was not only inefficient, but sometimes completely careless and unmindful of his duties. He would carry out his master's commands in a way that would upset even the

most calm and generous of hosts. The visitors of high repute became increasingly
alarmed at the disrespect that the servant
showed his master, even at the most important social gatherings. He constantly
attracted attention with his disheveled
dress, rude behavior and his highly
unnerving clumsiness in serving the guests
their food and drink.

Amazingly, the faithful master was never
annoyed, but always treated his servant in a
most sympathetic manner. One night the
servant dropped a wine decanter which shattered into ten thousand pieces, sending
shards of broken crystal in all directions
and a spate of red wine spilling over the
expensive carpets. His guests were flabber-
gasted to see the patient merchant smiling
at the servant and giving him only words of
encouragement, as the entire household
rushed to clean up the mess.

Unable to bear this any longer, one of the
guests remonstrated loudly with the
merchant, demanding that he dismiss the
servant immediately. The merchant replied,
"My dear sir, I greatly appreciate your
advice, given in friendship and with the
best intention. I know that you wish only for
my prosperity and I am aware that my reputation is being ruined and that my business is
suffering. But I keep this servant on the
very ground of his obstinacy and unfaithful-
ness. By virtue of his bad conduct he is very

precious to me. The disturbance and disgust
that he creates around him is my greatest
possession."

In the silence which settled over his
glittering guests in their opulent
surroundings, the master continued: "He is
the only man in the world who unfailingly
disobeys my commands, and who says things
that are derogatory and uncomplimentary to
me. All others with whom I come in contact
are continuously pleasant, loving and
gentle in their efforts to avoid my displea-
sure, and if I did not have his company I
would certainly fall prey to the various
sins of this high-flown society life.

"I am by nature a poet and a philosopher,
but my father, and indeed my entire family,
forced me to support them by continuing in
this family business. I cursed them for
their insistence, but as time passed I took
up the challenge of my worldly task. I then
began to see that every difficulty that came
my way in tending my business, with all of
its social responsibilities, was in reality
a blessing in disguise. It strengthened
something deep within me, and that divine
and mystical presence, about which I had
merely dreamt when I was a young poet, began
to fill my life of duty with an ineffable
peace.

"Because I am rich, I am visited by new
temptations every day; but the Lord, whom I
love above all else, has, in His infinite

compassion, given me the key to His kingdom.
He has sent me this wicked servant who tests
my spirit, hones my patience and destroys my
appetite for praise. I am compelled to
wrestle unremittingly with my lower nature,
and having conquered new ground each day,
step by step, I remain free: free from the
nightmare of consideration of other
peoples' opinions about me, free from the
delusion that my well-being depends upon
anything or anyone else but that blessed
Friend dwelling in my heart.

"In this way I have discovered that my
greatest fortune is this wicked servant of
mine."

Hearing this, his guests quietly departed,
some never to return again. Those who did,
however, came not to tax the merchant's
hospitality, but to hear his wisdom, while
the wicked servant continued in his cherished ways.

The End

I pondered over what Lesley was trying to say about
himself through this story.

By 1993 Lesley's life had been thrown into turmoil
and confusion as a result of six years of having become
more or less institutionalized on death row. He had set
up for himself a sort of monastic lifestyle within the con-
fines of his limited existence. However, his inner life was
flowering.

On 10 January 1995 he had written:

Dear Joy:

Thank you so much for your many cards and letters. They have been a great inspiration in my time of troubles. I am deeply grieved at having not written sooner, but shortly after my second execution date was stayed my appeal moved into its ultimate "win or lose" phase and my attorneys and I have been focusing all of our time and energy on winning. To do any less would be tantamount to suicide. I'm sure that you understand my position. It does seem, though, that our efforts haven't been completely in vain for we have unearthed proof of gross misconduct by the prosecutor in presenting my case to the jury. Perhaps enough to at least warrant a new trial. However, this decision is still in the hands of the appeal courts and probably won't be resolved for some time yet. I shall endeavor to do a better job of keeping you updated as the drama deepens!

As I look over your letters, it becomes obvious that I'm not going to be able to address all of the issues which you've written about. So, with your leave, I'll pick and choose a bit, hoping that I can catch up more thoroughly in my next communication.

You speak of death in almost all of your letters. This is quite understandable considering my position and the recent loss of your beloved father. I know from my own experience that no words can really console

at the passing of such a one. But as words
are the only tools available to me, please
accept my deepest sympathy in this matter
and be assured that he is experiencing the
rewards of a truly virtuous life at this
very moment.

In your letter of September the 4th you
tell me that death is an enormous mystery.
And so it is for almost everyone on earth.
But this is only so because they are yet an
enormous mystery unto themselves! Please
allow me to explain what I mean by this. It
is the unanimous holding of the world's
religions that the soul is the center of our
being and the seat of our awareness. And that
this soul has "fallen," or temporarily
inhabits and animates a body made of inert
matter. Thereby enabling the soul to
interact with the rest of God's creation.
However, if this holding is correct, then
why are we not equally able to perceive both
the things of the body and things of the
spirit? Simply because the senses naturally
flow outward and the Kingdom of Heaven is
within. Have you ever considered the possibility that under certain circumstances the
senses could be turned in upon themselves,
revealing the realm of the Spirit? We would
know for sure that we're immortal then
wouldn't we? Letting thine eye become single
is the key. More on this next time.

In one of your more recent letters you said
that you would love to come for a visit.

Well, I would like nothing better myself. So if you can find the time, I will be happy to provide the way. Yes, I am completely serious about this. I still have quite a sum of money left after my various legal expenses and I can't imagine a better way of spending a bit of it. Also, I have discussed the idea with a minister friend who has been visiting me regularly for over seven years. Her name is Kathy Cox. You may have heard of her work through some of the anti-death penalty publications. Her knowledge of Texas death row is encyclopedic as she has been ministering to the inmates here for nearly fifteen years. Kathy says that she would be more than happy to make the necessary arrangements for your visit. And we would both very much like for you to see firsthand how things are here. Please let me know something on this as soon as you can as my time may be short.

Find enclosed one of the photographs you sent to me when we first began corresponding. If my guess is correct, it contains the images of some of the kids who have written to me. Would you please identify the members of your group so that I can perhaps match a face to the name on some of the letters I'm attempting to answer?

Well, I had better close this epistle and get it posted. Thank you again for having the faith to continue writing even though I didn't answer for so long. Your letters

helped to maintain my sanity. Now that the
pressure is off for a bit I'd like to do some
catching up. So take good care of yourself
and let me hear from you again soon.

Almost to the very end, Lesley always hoped and
believed in the possibility that his case would be properly
resolved. From the very beginning there had been a huge
question mark over who had pulled the trigger in the kid-
napping in which the beautiful forty-two-year-old
Rebecca Patton had been killed. Lesley had been convicted on the word of a criminal who had recently been
released from ten years in jail. Lesley had consistently
maintained his innocence. It was only much later on that
I was to learn all the details of the case. It was never sub-
ject-matter for our correspondence.

In this letter above, some of Lesley's Eastern-inspired
philosophy was emerging. Although widely versed in
Christian theology, philosophy and the New Testament,
he remained to the end rooted in a sort of Eastern mysticism based on the teachings of the "Sant Mat" school.

"Sant Mat" means "Path of the Masters" and goes
back to the dawn of recorded history. It has been taught
in its present form since the time of Kabir in the four-
teenth century. Kabir proclaimed the essential unity of
all religions and the possibility and necessity of the union
of the soul with its Creator during one's lifetime.

The present chief guru is Ajaib Singh. He teaches that
everyone should have love for all and should meditate.
We can see God and receive his love if we go inward. If we
meditate, love will start manifesting in us. Meditation
and love go side by side. There must be love and respect
for all. Material riches are nothing. What is important is

achieving oneness with God. It is a hard road that requires strict discipline.

Lesley was aware that a similar teaching is reflected in the New Testament. For example: "I am the one who reproves and disciplines all those he loves: so repent in real earnest. Look, I am standing at the door, knocking. If one of you hears me calling and opens the door, I will come in to share his meal, side by side with him." (Revelation 3:19–20)

In his letter, Lesley had referred to a possible visit. Unfortunately, circumstances had made his generous offer impossible to take up. It was postponed only to recur in 1997.

From 1995 onward, Lesley was busier than ever. He already had so much going on in his life with all his intellectual and artistic pursuits, but now he was to be overwhelmed with legal work—not only for himself, but for so many others on death row. Lesley always seemed to be thinking of other people.

On 20 October 1995 there was a short letter sharing something that was extremely bad news for all death row prisoners in the U.S.A.:

```
Dear Joy:

Thank you very much for all of the cards,
letters, and photograph you've sent during
the past several months. I'm sorry that I
haven't written, but things have not been
going too well for those of us here on death
row. As I mentioned some time back, attor-
neys for the indigent death row inmates
(which make up the majority of the DR popula-
tion, both male and female) have been
furnished in the past by a government funded
```

organization called the Texas Resource
Center. Due to the increasingly conservative political climate here in the U.S., our
legislature has voted to cease funding for
not only the Texas Resource Center, but all
of the similar organizations across the U.S.
So as of October 1st, approximately 1,500
death row inmates across the U.S. were
without any form of legal representation.
Certain states (including Texas) are making
efforts to supply counsel through alterna-
tive means, but I fear for the quality of the
legal work. I have been fortunate in that
this disaster did not affect my situation.
The attorneys from the Resource Center who
were handling my case, though they have
moved on to other law firms, have agreed to
continue to represent me until my case is
resolved one way or another. However, many
others here have not been so fortunate—and
some of them illiterate or with no knowledge
of the legal system. So day after day a
number of us have been writing letters to
attorneys all across the U.S. trying to find
representation for those who can't write or
don't know how to deal with the courts. We
haven't been very successful, but have found
several highly talented lawyers willing to
work pro bono. Our quest continues. Everything else seems to be going well. I can't
say much about the weather here as I've been
too busy to notice what it's doing. I was
very pleased to hear that you and the kids

are doing well. Please let them know that I haven't forgotten them and will write as soon as this emergency passes. In the meantime, take good care of yourself and always remember God, for He always remembers us.

Sincerely;
Lesley Gosch

Thank you for your prayers!

After this letter, there was again a two-year gap in our contact. I sent a few letters, but did not receive any replies. I later learned that this was not only because of Lesley's intense legal activity; he was also going through a severe bout of depression. He became so despondent that he couldn't even do his artwork. He would pick it up only to abandon it after a few moments saying, "What's the use? I'm going to die anyway."

I am now so very aware of how important it is to keep on writing even if the replies are infrequent or stop altogether. There is always a reason for it.

What happened next came as a total and unexpected surprise . . .

2

The Invitation

Nearly two years later, on a hot day in August, this card arrived at my home in Rhos-on-Sea, North Wales:

August 11th 1997

Dear Joy:

Please forgive me for not writing, but my deteriorating legal situation has been consuming all of my time. Nevertheless, you and the children are in my thoughts and in my prayers daily. If there is any one thing that I would ask of you, it would be for you to come for a visit and be a witness to the world of what is happening here. My offer to pay your way still stands. But please come soon for my time is short.

```
Take good care of yourself and give my
regards to the kids!
```

The card portrayed an exquisite dragonfly with gossamer wings, against a white background engraved with water lilies. I marveled at the intricate work of art before me. I was bowled over. So, after all these years of slowly getting to know Lesley Gosch, the state of Texas was really and truly going to kill him. All this time I had blocked the thought of it from my mind. Surely not Lesley? Not the fine person I had gradually been discovering. I was deeply shocked. But if it were true . . . then how could I refuse this touching invitation? My cousin Dulcie was staying with me at the time: "I think you must go, Joy. You may always regret it if you don't."

Oh yes, I must go. It was one of those rare occasions in life when you know with absolute certainty what your response must be.

I realized that the decision was made. However, I could not envisage making this unique trip on my own. Who could I ask to join me? Who on earth would want to go to Texas death row with me? Immediately one name came to mind—Margôt Aczel, an old school friend who had recently returned with John, her husband, to live in North Wales after many years in Surrey. Margôt has a kind, generous and compassionate nature and is an experienced traveler. I picked up the phone:

"Hi, Margôt . . . how would you like to come to Texas with me?"

"Texas?!" I could hear the amazement in her voice.

"Yes, Texas! To visit my friend on death row. He thinks he will be executed soon."

"Of course I'll come! I can go shopping while you visit him!"

At first this seemed a great idea. Margôt loves shopping so she would be getting pleasure from the trip. She wouldn't just be hanging around waiting for me. Then suddenly a flash of pure inspiration came. Perhaps Lesley had a friend who would appreciate a visit from Margôt? I put the thought to her:

"Margôt, how would *you* like to visit a death row prisoner?"

"Yes, that would be fine! Why not?"

We dashed off a letter to Lesley, and by return of post Margôt was given a name: Ted. She had to send her credentials to the prison immediately so that they could be processed, enabling Margôt to be put on Ted's visiting list. "Ted" at this time was just a name. Little could either of us have guessed, in that hot August week, the extent to which Margôt's life as well as my own would be permanently affected by this forthcoming visit. Within one week, Margôt had said "Yes" twice.

So that was it. All we had to do now was to plan the trip as quickly as possible. Was this really happening?

During the three weeks that followed, my thoughts became focused on Lesley. When a person is about to die they become uniquely precious. This man was not terminally ill, he was waiting to be killed. I felt sick to the stomach and hovered from disbelief to the realization that it could indeed be happening.

From that time onward, Margôt and I were to feel that we had embarked on one huge learning curve.

3

Huntsville, Texas

The countdown to Texas was on. I made all the necessary arrangements such as booking my cat into a cattery
and informing everyone that I would be absent from my
various commitments for ten days. Margôt and I also had
to think about what to take with us. It was going to be
very hot so for the most part it would be just T-shirts and
jeans.

In between all the practicalities and preparations I
would turn again and again to the letters. Lesley Gosch
seemed to me to be a very impressive person. I couldn't
wait to meet him.

By the end of September, Margôt and I were touching
down at Houston. My first ever visit to the U.S.A!
Margôt had been several times before, though never to
Texas. We now had to cope with jet lag and the task of
finding our way to a car rental company, and then driving to the Day's Inn where we had a good night's rest.

The name Huntsville filled us both with a sense of fore-boding, so the next morning we spent a little time look-ing around Houston before setting off.

It was good, though, to leave the busy city behind and be out on the freeway. Ironically, the nearer we got to Huntsville the more beautiful the countryside became. Yet still reluctant to arrive at this "killing town," we stopped for a couple of coffees en route. Eventually the signpost "Huntsville" was staring us in the face. I felt my stomach turn over, and Margôt seemed to be feeling something similar. There was no way to go but forward.

The Texas roads are truly amazing, they just stretch on and on and are easy to drive on—once us Brits have remembered to use the right-hand side! Suddenly in the distance we saw a huge white statue looming. As we drew nearer we saw that it was of Sam Houston, the founding father of the city. It was taller than the tallest trees—never had we seen such an enormous statue.

In no time at all we were in Huntsville, a small, quiet and not unpleasant town, the sort often seen featured as the backdrop to films. We had arranged to stay at Hospi-tality House, a Baptist-run facility for friends and fami-lies of people visiting death row and other prisons. We found it easily: 912 Tenth Street. We had no idea what sort of place it would be. "If we don't like it we can always find an inn," said Margôt. However, we were most agree-ably surprised. It was a pleasant house with a large gar-den. We drove up and parked the car. As soon as the door opened and we were greeted by the pastor, Bob Norris, we knew that any apprehensions we had were ground-less. As we entered we found ourselves in a spacious, comfortable lounge. Behind it was a well-stocked and spotlessly clean kitchen. To the right and left of the lounge were small passageways leading to two dormitories. Each room in the dormitory contained four bunk beds separated by a half wall and a curtain. The rooms, beds and facilities were basic, but absolutely adequate. That we were sleeping in bunk beds did not matter at all. What was important was the atmosphere, which was quite wonderful. The place had been built ten years previously, in forty-eight hours, by 220 Baptist men.

Each time we were to come back to Hospitality House after visiting death row was truly to feel like a homecoming. The place was full of peace and love, a place of sanity and comfort. Huntsville has thirty-three thousand inhabitants, the majority of whom earn their living from working in one way or another in the town's many prisons. There are sixty-nine thousand prisoners and more prisons are being built. Death row itself houses the condemned, an average of two being executed by lethal injection each month, even if their guilt may remain questionable.

The slogan of Hospitality House is "Help for Hurting Families," and it was moving to see this in practice and to become part of it. To "waste" a little time sitting around in the lounge (there is no television) proved to be most rewarding. This was how we came into contact with the deep pain of mothers and other family members visiting their loved ones on death row or in other prisons. Hearing their heart-rending stories helped us to build up a picture of life for the less advantaged in the richest country in the world. We concluded that in this culture even the rich live in constant fear of losing what they have. In a country where there are more guns than people, this situation seems to us to be a recipe for disaster. And there is plenty of disaster as the prisons and death row are there to testify.

At Hospitality House we uncovered layer upon layer of human sorrow and broken hearts. We wept with mothers, sisters and friends. But that is not the whole picture, for there was laughter too. It is a unique community where, for the short time that you are there, you all feel as one, whether through sharing verbally or in the deep silence of understanding—and sometimes even by keeping a respectful distance. There is also a tiny chapel which is in frequent use. It contains a wooden cross, a table holding a large Bible, a small sofa and a small writing desk with paper, pens and, significantly, an ever-refilled box of tissues. The chapel is frequently used as a room not only for praying in, but also for weeping in. I used it for both when I got my first bad news about Lesley.

From the very first, our association with Hospitality House was a blessed one. Not only was the atmosphere lovingly charged, but all our practical needs were discreetly catered for. One of the loveliest memories is of Bob preparing delicious warm rolls for us each morning, as well as his superb pots of freshly brewed coffee. Not to mention the abundance of fruit and cereals. Everything was done with maximum love and minimum fuss.

Firmly settled in at Hospitality House, we had three days before our visits began. By an amazing coincidence, a friend of Margôt's from her Surrey days, Gloria, was now living in Houston. She came over for the weekend, staying with her friend Sheila, who happened to live in Huntsville. We all spent a pleasant weekend together, shopping, chatting and visiting Sheila's house up in the woodland area.

We used the shopping trips as an opportunity to speak about the death penalty. Shop assistants seemed to like our English accents and would tell us of their enormous sorrow over the death of Princess Diana. They would ask if we were over on vacationing, to which we would reply, "Well, actually we're visiting friends on death row."

"Wow!" was a frequent response.

And so an informal discussion would follow. Most of the women would admit to having ambivalent feelings about the death penalty, saying things like: "If it were my son who'd killed someone, I'd definitely be against it. If my child had been killed, I'd surely be for it."

They were all very nice to us and would often add things like: "I admire what you're doing."

The two days we spent with Gloria ended with all of us attending Mass at the only Catholic church in Huntsville. The liturgy was beautiful and the people very friendly. We couldn't, however, help feeling sad that no mention was made, no prayer offered (at least while we were there), for those being killed in their midst.

4

Visits, Vigils and Executions

It was Monday, and at last we could start looking forward to the long-awaited visits to our prisoners. From Wales we had arranged for our trip to fall in both September and October, believing that in this way we would be allowed eight hours of visiting for each month, sixteen hours altogether. However, on arrival, we were informed by telephone that because the planned visits fell in one and the same week, we could only have eight hours. That was a very big disappointment. The first visits would be on Tuesday, so we had one more day to wait and more time to fill. We were going through the motions of doing ordinary things like shopping, but I think really we were both doing our best to protect each other from the underlying tension we were feeling at the prospect of visiting death row.

That evening there was to be an execution down at The Walls prison in Huntsville. There had been one on the first evening we arrived, the night we were staying over in Houston. Another one was scheduled for Tuesday. Three executions during the week of our visit. Even by Texas standards, that was unusual.

We had no idea where The Walls prison was, but we decided to find out. We planned to take part in the vigil that we had heard always takes place at an execution. It was quite busy at Hospitality House as the evening before there had been a seminar for about twenty women whose husbands were due to be released in the near future. One of these, Mary, was sharing a dormitory with us. She was a gentle person with a lovely southern drawl, a devout Christian who had absolute trust in God regarding her future. It was very touching to see how Mary and all the other women would be up at about 5:30 A.M. on visiting days. An hour's attention to hair, make-up and clothes, and they were all transformed into southern belles. They were beautiful, all of them, totally devoted to their men. One could only hope and pray for them that things would go well in all their futures. These men were not death row men: they were what is known as "Population"—that is, inmates of other prisons. For them there is always hope of parole. In Texas there is no life sentence without the chance of parole. If the death penalty is abolished, there will be the danger of the state introducing life-without-parole sentences.

After breakfast we decided to explore Huntsville. We were told the weather was cool, but it was still in the high nineties! Driving around, we discovered a charming soda parlor where we cooled off—a place that we were to frequent in the following days and on our second visit. In that heat, you just don't walk anywhere and you don't rush. Quite something for me, as I tend to be a walker and a fast mover! However, these breaks were also an invaluable time for Margôt and me to share our reflections and evaluate all that we were seeing, hearing and experiencing.

We had heard a rumor that death row prisoners' arts and crafts were actually sold at The Walls prison. It was not very hard to find, because the walls were so high. We stopped and gazed for some moments, trying to come to grips with the reality of what went on within. We looked up at the towers and saw the guards with their huge rifles. We found it incredibly hard to comprehend. Feeling none too safe, we nevertheless ventured toward what looked like a main entrance. As we proceeded, it felt increasingly eerie. Suddenly we saw a young woman who appeared to be a receptionist and we asked if it were true that prisoners' craft-work was sold there. She said that she had never heard of anything like that, but telephoned a superior. A couple of minutes later an older woman came down and asked us what we wanted. We repeated the question. She looked us up and down and told us that nothing like that had been done for a good twenty years. She seemed suspicious of us, and later we reflected that in all probability she thought we were journalists, it being an execution day.

We drove around The Walls once or twice, just taking in the scene and trying to come to terms with the fact that at 6:00 P.M. we would be there as a person was executed: put down like a sick animal. Execution is much worse than that though. The last time I was at the vet's a lady brought her old cat to be put down. He was purring happily, blissfully unaware of what was soon to happen. He was secure in her arms, loved totally. Our friends who suffer execution have no loving arms around them, for physical contact is barred absolutely. I have met and spoken with mothers whose sons have been executed after twenty-three years, and never once in all that time have they been allowed to touch them. Moreover, unlike an animal, the man on death row "dies" over and over again before the lethal shot finally kills him. The knowledge that he'll be executed is with him each day as he wakes, each night before he sleeps, and during every moment of each day.

In the afternoon we decided to visit the Prison Museum—even against our better judgement. Why should we encourage the morbid pride that Huntsville takes in the prisons that provide so many of its inhabitants with employment? In the end we paid our two dollars each out of sheer curiosity. The museum was divided into two areas: the "old days" with the electric chair in a place of high honor, and the "new"—pictures of modern prisoners on death row and Population prisoners. Many of the photos were very demeaning to those on death row. A retired teacher ran the place. I asked her if she was embarrassed by people coming from all over the world and learning about what goes on in Huntsville's prisons. Non-smiling and defensive, she assured us that she was not: "Why should I be?"

She was just doing her job . . .

I asked her: "How do the people of Huntsville feel about prisoners regularly being killed in the center of their town?"

"They are very busy," she answered, "they don't think about it."

They don't think about it. What, I wondered, would happen if they *did* think about it?

After the visit to the prison museum we felt the need to touch base at Hospitality House, that haven of peace and sanity. A short siesta, time to freshen up and the inevitable cup of coffee, and we were ready, as far as one can be ready, to be at our first execution. Subdued, we drove down to The Walls. It was 5:30 P.M. Executions take place at 6:00 P.M.

Everything looked so normal. In this quiet green town people were starting to go home from work. The sky was deep Texan blue. The birds were singing high in the beautiful trees of a large detached house, home of The Walls' Warden. Inside the prison, people were preparing poisons to kill a man. Others were preparing to strap him down. Others would soon be politely escorting the witnesses to the death chamber: six members of the victim's family and six of the executee's friends or family. And outside we waited, watching the hands on the big prison clock move: 5:35, 5:40, 5:45 . . . and still the birds sang.

We chat quietly with others who have gathered. Margôt moves across to the other side of the road to help hold up a huge banner that reads "TEXAS STOP THE EXECUTIONS." Other banners say things like "MURDER IN PROGRESS," "THOSE WITH THE CAPITAL DON'T GET THE PUNISHMENT," "JOBS NOT JAILS," and "EXECUTION IS NOT THE SOLUTION."

The prison clock ticks: 5:50, 5:55, 6:00 P.M. The clock strikes. One, two, three, four, five, six. Has he had the first injection? And now the fatal ones? One to collapse the lungs and one to stop the heart. Who of his family are watching? God be with them now. And the victim's family. Yes, they have suffered horribly. They think that seeing this man die will finally take away some of their pain and make them feel better. We have learned, though, that rarely does this happen, probably not ever. Revenge eats away the inner fibers of one's being and often produces serious ill health. Forgiveness, on the other hand, has been proved to be life-giving and freeing, enabling those who choose that way to truly go forward with their lives.

A deep hush has fallen upon us all. Those who are believers have moved into silent or softly spoken prayer. I can hear one person praying in tongues, oh so softly. This person, I was later to discover, was Betty Mathews, a remarkable Texan whose life is almost entirely devoted to visiting death row prisoners. I see the handkerchief lifted to her eyes as the tears fall. She has been here so many times. Where does she find the strength? Silence. Is he dead yet? We know that it is all over when we see the witnesses being led down some steps into an inner courtyard of the prison. The two groups, six friends or family of the victim, six of the person being executed, have been kept entirely separate from each other. They never meet.

I love that famous quote of Sr. Helen Prejean, author of *Dead Man Walking*: "If killing is wrong, how can it be right to kill a man to show that killing is wrong." I do not know who was killed on that Monday evening as Huntsville's inhabitants drove past on their journeys home. Margôt and I were still very new in Huntsville, but we were learning fast.

At about 8:30 P.M. we arrived back at Hospitality House to be met by Pastor Bob. "Sister Joy, there has been a phone call for you; I'm afraid it's bad news." My heart raced. For a split second I thought my parents were still alive and that one of them had died.

"It's Lesley's lawyer. He wants you to phone him."

Oh no, I think, they're going to kill him. Tomorrow maybe?

Bob hands me the phone. I dial the number he holds in front of me.

"Hello, Raoul?"

"Hi! I'm really so sorry to have to tell you this. They have taken Lesley away to San Antonio to receive his execution date. It's 350 miles away." He went on: "Lesley asked me to tell you how bad he feels about this. He's more concerned about you than about himself."

Raoul lives in Austin so I didn't talk for long on the phone. I told him that we'd do all in our power to get to San Antonio.

We sat down and tried to face our dilemma. Tomorrow, our visits are due to start. Lesley is in San Antonio. I won't be going to death row. But Margôt is scheduled to visit Ted, Lesley's friend. She will be going to death row. I won't be.

I looked at Margôt, who was the one who bore the brunt of the driving. "What shall we do about Lesley?"

"We go to San Antonio!"

But how could we go to San Antonio *and* enable Margôt to visit Ted? It seemed the only solution was this: Margôt would visit Ted for four hours the next day, after which we would drive southwest to San Antonio. It was going to be tough, but it was decided. I don't think either of us slept much that night. Margôt—who, after all, initially only came to accompany me on this trip—was about to go alone to death row (fifteen miles from Huntsville) to meet a convicted murderer she had never even exchanged a letter with. And I was to wait at home at Hospitality House, and hope that somehow we would make it to San Antonio and find Lesley. How was he feeling? What had his trip been like?

Margôt was extremely apprehensive about her first visit to death row. Whatever were we caught up in? San Antonio seemed so far away.

The morning came at last. At 6:00 A.M. I got up and made Margôt a cup of tea. Like all the others she dressed very carefully for her visit. Luckily, a young German family were also visiting that morning so she was able to follow them in the car.

I felt really sad and lonely after they had all left, so I got busy packing our things ready to set off for San Antonio in the afternoon. I took our sheets to be washed and made the beds ready for the next visitors. We didn't expect to come back to Hospitality House as it would save time to drive straight to Houston from San Antonio.

I had been longing for an opportunity to be quite alone to collect my thoughts and pray a little. This was the opportunity. I went to the chapel. I loved this little room: the large cross, the table, the Bible which that day was open at the Sermon on the Mount. I read through the Beatitudes and then sat down on the sofa. All the emotions we had experienced since our arrival seemed to surface and I found myself shedding a few tears about the sorrow we were witnessing all around us: the women whose men were in prison, the men on death row, those who had been executed, and those—like Lesley—who had it all to come; and somehow for Jesus himself who went through all this, as did his friends, his mother and the women who surrounded him. The tears flowed and I felt better afterward; I then sat at the desk and wrote a few notes.

It was that morning that I met Maggie. Maggie had returned to Hospitality House five months after having witnessed the execution of her son, Billy Jo, the previous Easter. It was hard for her to return, but she felt she had to visit her son's friends at Ellis One (death row) as they had been so supportive to her. Billy Jo had been killed just two years after her husband's death, and after twenty-three years on death row. Her son had left behind a daughter, so at least Maggie has her grand-daughter.

Like so many of the men who have spent years on death row, Billy Jo had completely turned his life around. But on Texas death row there is no mercy. One of the very important lessons we learnt at Huntsville is how the death penalty not only kills one individual, but causes immense suffering to so many others, the friends and family of the person executed. Maggie is a gentle woman who could be anyone's granny. I knew then that I would always think of her on Good Fridays. She told me she found great support in her church and all the people there. If only those who authorize executions would open their hearts into windows of awareness of what they set in motion each time they kill a person. If they did, they simply would not be able to do it. "Father, forgive them . . ."

At last it was 1:00 P.M.; the bags were packed and standing ready near the front door. I was aching to be on my way to San Antonio to fulfil my mission of meeting Lesley.

At 1:10 the door opened and in walked Margôt and the lovely young German family. All looked elated and I knew instantly that Margôt's visit had been a huge success. I was delighted and wanted to hear every detail—but not until we were on the road to San Antonio! However, as we had a cup of coffee and a banana, it dawned on me that we would not actually be going to San Antonio that day. Margôt was deeply, and beyond all expectation, moved by her visit with Ted. I knew there and then that I could not let her forgo her four hours of Wednesday's visits, not even if I had to have less time with Lesley. She had told Ted that she might not be able to go the next day because of what had happened to Lesley. He had been so gracious, telling her not to worry and that it was all in God's hands. We chatted it over with Pastor Bob and we felt it would be right to remake our beds and go calmly to San Antonio the following day, and this is in fact what happened.

Staying the extra night enabled us to go to that evening's execution. This time it was a tall, white-haired grand-father. Margôt had seen him in the visiting area at Ellis One that morning, and had met his family too. She told me how very dignified the man was and how distraught his family were. At the vigil I was with his cousin, two daughters and a son. The wife and other family members were with him in the death-room. One of his daughters had given birth just three days before. The other daughter was pregnant. The son was quiet, but I was somehow aware of an ice-cold anger within him. I chatted with his cousin as we stood on the grass in the beautiful evening sunshine. She told me executions are not as bad now as in the days of the electric chair. They were then carried out at midnight and the lights at Huntsville University would all go out until it was over; her daughter had been a student there in those days. When the clock struck six, she moved away and stood all alone behind a tree, weeping.

The following day we would be on our way to San Antonio, leaving the horrors of Huntsville behind for a few months.

5

Bexar County Jail, San Antonio

At last we were on the road after Margôt's second visit to Ted, which again had been extremely successful.

It was 2:00 P.M. and we had at least five hours of driving ahead of us in the heat of the Texas afternoon. Before leaving we had phoned the San Antonio county jail to find out how long I could spend with Lesley, to be told "half-an-hour." This was crazy, and I felt sure that if we spoke "sweetly" to the administration they would take pity on us. We stopped only once on the way, pressing relentlessly on until San Antonio was in sight.

San Antonio is a very large city. How would we find the county jail? We stopped on the outskirts and approached a fireman just returning from duty, asking if he knew where the Bexar county jail was. "It's right there, ma'am!" he said, pointing to a modern building just down the road. What a miracle to have found it so easily.

Somewhere inside that quite, pleasant-looking building was Lesley Gosch, the friend I had been writing to for the past five years.

We were directed to a waiting room upstairs and told to sit down. Looking around the room we noticed that there was not a single white face to be seen: the family members of the men in the county jail were all black or Hispanic, mostly the latter. They were very quiet: resigned and patient. They must have been worried too.

The county jails, I had been told, are very bad places, where those picked up from the streets are just dumped until their trials come up. They are herded together with no privacy. Lesley, of course, was different; he was down here from death row, Huntsville, and he was on "lockdown," in total isolation. As we sat there waiting, I pondered over a conversation I had had with Kathryn Cox the evening before. Kathryn is the woman minister who had known Lesley for a number of years and whom he trusted and respected enormously. Not only had she spoken in glowing terms of Lesley's many gifts, she had also told me that she was convinced he was not the person who killed Rebecca Patton. If this were true, it added another dimension to the events that were now unfolding so dramatically in Lesley's life.

The officer at the desk was a kind-looking black American. I told him my story, how I had come all the way from North Wales to see Lesley Gosch. I pleaded with him to let us have more than half-an-hour together. He smiled, and promised me he would do his best. He did, in fact, manage to give me two hours with Lesley.

Eventually the number of the booth where the visit was to take place was called and I moved swiftly over there. My heart was pounding. Lesley was led in, handcuffed, a short man, wearing thick dark-rimmed glasses. He was wearing the bright orange uniform of the Bexar county jail.

As I moved toward the booth there was no smile of recognition. He had the unconnected look of a blind man. He had never mentioned his blindness in his letters. He later explained to me that although he was registered blind, with his special glasses he was able to see just six inches in front of him. It wasn't until we sat down, that he could see me. He explained to me how his blindness and other handicaps had been caused by an explosion while doing a chemistry experiment during his school-days. And then our troubles began. We could not hear each other! We tried, but to no avail. "Don't worry," I said, trying to conceal my anguish, "I'll sort it out." I dashed out to the kind officer and explained our predicament. "I'll move you to another booth," was his response.

Poor Lesley. Into the handcuffs again. Next booth. Sure that all was bound to be well now, I began speaking, but when he responded I could hear only with great difficulty. Hot and very tired, I could have burst into tears at this point. I returned to the officer.

"I am so sorry," he said, "I'm afraid I can't give you a telephone because Gosch is on lockdown."

Words cannot describe how I felt at seeing Lesley being treated so shamefully. What must it be like to have so little control over your life that you can't walk one yard without handcuffs? And not even having the privileges of those locked up in the rest of the county jail.

There was nothing else to do but to try and make the best of this dreadful situation. We had to make a supreme effort in order to communicate at all, so we both got into a crouching position, our bodies doubled over in an extremely painful way so that our lips were practically touching the glass. Catching a few sounds, we did the rest by lip-reading. It was a very great strain physically for both of us. To have come so far only to find ourselves in this predicament, and for just two hours! Two hours of excruciating pain was tough. I gazed at the face in front of me. He looked worn out, but he began to smile. This was indeed a very special moment.

Somehow we did communicate. Lesley began by thanking me for coming. He said how very sorry he was that it had to be this way, and how he wished he could have entertained me, as planned, on death row. He explained that it was so unnecessary for him to be there in San Antonio. It was simply so that the judge could be seen on television handing out a death warrant. In the current political climate these performances help to enhance a judge's popularity.

Margôt and I have both found that the topic of over-riding concern and interest to our friends on death row is spirituality. Lesley began almost at once telling me of his love for the Christian and Eastern mystical writers. It had been a major experience for him when he realized that, on reading the mystics, the things they described fitted almost exactly the type of experiences he had had on death row as he progressed steadily through his relentless "dark night" existence. I felt that he didn't want to waste a second of this stringently rationed time.

He went on to tell me that he was feeling very tired as the journey to San Antonio had been rough. On the bench-warranting journeys prisoners are shackled at the feet as well as at the wrists. Margôt and I had traveled in an air-conditioned car. Lesley had been in a truck, on a small hard bench.

He told me that the cell at this jail was four-by-four-foot and was like a butcher's refrigerator. For some obscure reason, the air-conditioning is turned up extra high for death row prisoners.

I asked him how he passed the many hours in those conditions. He told me that he had brought with him a very good book on the Beatitudes. The Beatitudes! My mind went straight back to the previous day's hour in the chapel at Hospitality House. "Blessed are the poor." Who could be more poor than Lesley and all the other 3,300 death row inmates across the U.S.A.? They have lost so much, if not everything, that the rest of us take for granted. It is this loss that leads so many of them to know their need of God and in turn to be so surely touched by him. How often Jesus made it plain in his teachings that it was the lost, the sick, the lonely, the *little* ones, he came to save. This special poverty of theirs makes *us* feel very humble. Through them we too are deeply touched and made more whole by the God of infinite love. The week before we had left for Texas, a Jesuit friend, Gerard W. Hughes, had written: "I do hope you can go. Nothing happens by chance! Don't be afraid—just be your-self—and that will help him enormously! And may Love direct your steps." Remembering this, and in spite of the discomfort, I tried to relax and just "be."

Lesley went on to say how hard it was being away from Ellis One, not only because often the guards would "trash" personal possessions during a prisoner's absence, but also because on his return he would find that some people, friends, had been executed while he was away. "You never know who's going to be next." He reflected that it must be like that in times of war.

He told me about the painting of a snow tiger he was working on and which was to be for me, and that he was making more musical instruments. One of them, a very special flute, was to be another gift for me; he intended sending it as soon as possible.

Lesley apologized for the periods when he had stopped writing, explaining that when he felt low it was hard to write. It was the same with his artistic projects. Sometimes he would go for days without doing anything, thinking, "What's the point? I'll soon be dead." But he always tried to overcome these dark moods.

I told him that I was sorry that there had been times when I too had dropped off in the correspondence, adding that after this meeting I would never do that again. Actually *being* there with Lesley made me realize how important it is to be consistent in one's correspondence. I now know more than ever before just how important letters are to death row prisoners. One prisoner, Garry, was later to tell me that he used to send away for junk mail just so that he received something from the postman. Many of the poems written by prisoners emphasize the significance of letters in their lives.

Lesley described how he, Ted and Garry, along with another friend, Cliff (executed 11 June 1998), would meet together whenever possible in their brief recreation period in order to discuss their prayer and their reading. They used to try to witness a little more openly, but now preferred to do it just by example. The four of them all tried to give much needed encouragement to each other, especially if one was going through a difficult time.

He talked to me about the terrible experience he had when he went to the death house on his first execution date. His feelings and thoughts were in turmoil. Before leaving that first time, he had opened his Bible at a passage where Jesus spoke of forgiveness. It was an illumination. At that moment he knew that he must, like Jesus, forgive his executioners. While sitting in the waiting room next to the death house, he told his executioners that he forgave them.

I asked him what their response was. He said they were shocked; no one had ever done that before.

He was given a stay of execution just twenty-eight minutes before he was due to be killed. A stay of execution usually comes in the form of a phone call from the lawyers. He told me that when he got back to his cell on Ellis One he felt as though he had been beaten all over with a baseball bat. He had lain on his bed and slept for twelve hours. That was in 1993.

I told him, "Lesley, you're a beautiful person."

This brought a smile. "Well, Sister Joy, I think you're a very loving person yourself."

I then heard him saying these words, so often spoken by the great saints and which he had made his own: "Love is all."

He asked me what I thought of death row. I told him I thought it was hateful to keep men in cages until the state decides to kill them, but that because of the many good people there, especially himself, it was in a way, for me, holy ground.

Lesley said to me that one day I would understand why it had to be this way: the chase to San Antonio and the difficulties of the visit. I reflected on this later; it certainly enabled me to see first-hand the awfulness of the unnecessary bench-warranting procedure. It was such a shock to see how the so-called most advanced nation in the world treats these poor forgotten men and women.

I thought of Lesley's card asking me to visit, so that I could "witness to the world about what is happening here." I said, "Lesley, you will never know all the repercussions that will follow on from your invitation to visit."

He smiled and said that it didn't matter, and that he didn't need to.

In the shadows I saw the guard approaching. The two hours were up. Lesley's last words were, "Perhaps you'll come back?" I didn't want to make a promise I wouldn't be able to keep. I gave him a big smile which I hoped was reassuring.

The guard was here. Lesley, with years of practice behind him, walked slowly backward to receive the handcuff. My last sight of him was as he raised his cuffed hand in a farewell gesture. I felt infinitely sad seeing him go like that. There would have been so much more talking to do. It seemed so cruel.

The visit was not as either of us would have wished, but it had been achieved. Margôt and I would surely return one day. My back was aching and I walked in a slightly dazed state to where Margôt was deep in conversation with a Mexican woman who was waiting to visit her son.

And so we left the county jail, San Antonio, behind us and drove off into the night. It was about 9:00 P.M. We hadn't eaten, but we wanted to drive as far as possible en route to Houston where we had to catch the plane at 4:00 P.M. the next day. At midnight we pulled up at an inn and were given a room with two wonderful, comfortable beds. We had been too tired to talk much on the journey. I didn't have to explain to Margôt the disappointment of the short and painful meeting with Lesley. She knew and understood all too well. It just made her all the more grateful for the eight hours she had with Ted.

The next morning, genuinely rested, we drove to Houston, took the car back to the car rental company, and were driven to the airport by a very kind senior citizen. He told us he was retiring that very day, not because he wanted to but, he explained, he could no longer bear the racism of the "yuppies" who worked in the firm and who treated the black drivers and porters as if they were nothing. He and his wife were retired teachers; he liked his job, but couldn't live with such disrespect. It seemed that everywhere we moved in Texas we uncovered so much sorrow.

And so at last we were homeward bound . . . while poor Lesley was still sitting in his cell in the Bexar county jail, San Antonio.

Ahead of us we had a two-hour wait in Paris where we walked right into a controlled bomb explosion. Margôt burst out laughing: "Well, that's *all* we need!" We didn't wait around to hear who had planted the bomb. We just left the area as fast as possible in our haste to meet two French friends who were waiting for us.

Manchester seemed like Paradise when the plane finally touched down! It was good to be on home ground. Back in North Wales, John, Margôt's husband, gave us a very warm welcome and was extremely happy to see that we had made it.

6

Between Visits

The first ones to hear our story properly and fully were Sister Piedad, a Spanish nun, and Paul Hunt, an Anglican vicar from the Midlands. Both were following a two-month course at Saint Beuno's, a Jesuit center of spirituality not far from my home. We had met before leaving for Texas and Paul had prayed over us, with special prayers for our visit to death row. That in itself had been a very special meeting: I had known Paul some thirty years earlier in Liverpool. I had been deeply impressed with his tremendous joy in the Lord. Piedad I count among my dearest sister friends. Although we had never lived in community together, we had followed a three-month course known as "the tertianship" at Frascati, near Rome, some fifteen or twenty years previously. We had not met in between, as she had always been in Kenya, Spain or the Philippines.

On our return from Texas, Paul and Piedad came over to Colwyn Bay. At Deganwy, Margôt's home, with the sea almost in the front garden, we sat for a full two hours. They were very good and patient listeners! That too was the day that the media began bursting into our lives. Our story had hit the headlines of the *Daily Post*, thanks to the very genuine interest of one of its chief reporters, Ian Lang, encouraged by his former chief features editor, Mr. Iorweth Roberts. Ian became deeply involved in Lesley's story and his possible fate. He went to endless trouble in contacting the San Antonio press and obtaining the first good photos of Lesley, which later were shown many times on television and appeared in various newspapers. Ian believed totally in Lesley's innocence and felt personally hurt at what was happening to him: "It's a system that churns people up and spits them out; it's an insult to our humanity." He demonstrated to me how impossible it would have been for Lesley to fire those fatal shots with his near-blindness and, to our surprise, his missing fingertips!

It was around this time that the following card arrived from Lesley:

```
Dear Joy:

I just arrived back at Ellis a couple of
hours ago and am frantically trying to get
caught up on everything. I just wanted to
write and tell you how much I enjoyed our all
too brief visit and again apologize for all
of the disappointments and inconveniences
you experienced while here. Perhaps we can
try it again in the future under less trying
circumstances. Yes, I received an execution
date as I thought I would—January 15th,
```

1998. At this point in time I don't know how
serious this date will be. It all depends on
which federal judge I draw when my attorneys
apply for my stay. If I draw a liberal judge,
a stay is assured. If I draw a conservative
judge, this could easily be my last date,
ever. I promise to keep you informed on this
as things develop. On the subject of trip
finances, I need you to write Kathy Cox and
let her know how much you're going to need to
cover your trip expenses. She takes care of
all of my business affairs. Well, that's
about all I can think of in my present
muddled mental state. Take care and try to
get a note to Kathy soon. I promise to write
more next week.

From the time of receiving this, Margôt and I felt very
troubled and concerned.

Lesley had asked that we witness to the world about
what was happening at Huntsville and now was our
opportunity. That day the telephone rang continuously,
and in the early evening reporters from Granada News
came over from Liverpool, not to mention Harlech Television (HTV) and BBC Wales. John Aczel was very generous indeed in allowing us to use his office for several
interviews.

The media interest continued for several weeks. We
did more radio broadcasts than we could count. We also
lost track of the numerous press articles and local TV
items. We were invited to Cardiff to speak on a *Woman's
Hour* program, and we went to Lyme Park, Buxton, to be
on a Sunday morning live religious program with Pam
Rhodes. With us on the *Woman's Hour* program was Ann

Widdecombe, former minister for prisons. Ann would be strongly in favor of bringing back the death penalty to the U.K. However, when we went to have a chat with her at Westminster she assured us that this will not happen. Sighs of relief!

Somewhere in the midst of all these activities we made another trip to London to speak to a gathering of the sisters of my order, the Missionary Sisters of Africa. They were a wonderful audience, one hundred percent with us.

Of course, everyday life had to go on too. For Margôt, this was mainly her family plus a Russian lady, Tanya, whom she cares for. Margôt's three sons have now gone their separate ways, but frequently return home. There is also Margôt's first little grand-daughter, Francesca, her pride and joy!

For me it was my work in the hospital of Glan Clwyd—where I am a member of the chaplaincy team—as well as the school chaplaincy work and activities in our parish that absorb a lot of my time. A couple of years ago a wonderful long-haired black and white cat walked into my life. He is a very relaxing companion!

Margôt and I continued to meet frequently. We found ourselves increasingly drawn into various aspects of death row work: not only the media input, but also giving talks—for instance to fourth, fifth and sixth graders in our North Wales comprehensive schools. Most days we telephoned each other and exchanged news. The most significant news of all during that time was Lesley's next execution date: 15 January 1998. When you write to a death row friend you know in your head that one of the dates will be the final one, but somehow it never quite registers. This date of 15 January was an extremely serious one, as Lesley was definitely at the end of his appeals. For the past three years he had two very good lawyers in

Raoul and Maurie, so we tried to keep our hopes up. We knew how hard they were working.

I thought about Lesley a great deal, saw him in my mind's eye back in that booth in San Antonio where he had told me that the only reason he had to make that terrible trip was so that the judge could be seen on television handing out an execution date.

On 4 November 1997 I received a long letter from Lesley:

Dear Joy:

Thank you for your letters of October the 11th, 15th, 18th, and 22nd. I always enjoy hearing from you. Please forgive me for not answering before now, but I have been spending all of my time doing legal research on issues I want my attorneys to include in my writ of habeas corpus. Under civil circumstances I could work at a leisurely pace, but getting this execution date has thrown everything into high gear. And not only for me, but for my lawyers as well.

In your letter of October the 11th, you asked if I was fond of animals. I love all life. For it is the presence of God's spirit in all things which give them life. Making every living thing just as much a child of God as we are. Therefore we should afford the same love and respect to animals we do to each other. For they are, in reality, our less capable brothers and sisters. And God has made it very plain to those who would heed His voice that their welfare is primary among our responsibilities as human beings. And that great blessings are in store for those with the courage to live this vision.

For example, on their whale rescue missions, Greenpeace members have experienced such blessings. The following story was related to me by one of my friends in this organization:

Placing themselves in the water between the whales and their attackers, Greenpeace members had just saved five whales from a Russian whaler. The next morning, one member celebrated by singing a song on deck. The music flowed out over the speakers across the churning waves.

Suddenly, five whales appeared on the horizon and approached the Greenpeace boat. Closer they came, breaching and blowing, moving in time with the music. They encircled the boat for nearly an hour. Then they pulled ahead, stopped, and lifted their massive heads out of the water, their large eyes level with the boat as it passed.

The crew stood silent on deck. "It was as though the whales were saluting us," my friend said. "The whales were saluting us. It was a conscious and deliberate action on their part."

Then the whales sounded and vanished beneath the sea, surfacing again far off on the horizon. And as the crew stood watching, a brief shower passed and a rainbow appeared above the whales. Was this incident merely chance, or God proclaiming the brotherhood of all life?

Joy, in your letter of October the 22nd, you indicated that a reporter was interested in doing a story about the situation here. Definitely go ahead with it. I can't possibly see how such a story could jeopardize my getting a stay of execution. Even if it did, I still want the story told! Don't get me wrong, becoming a martyr is the last thing I want, but so much evil exists in the world today simply because no one is willing to do what it takes to drag it, kicking and screeching, into the light. So even though the decision concerning the article has been reached without my attorney's input, you can still check on progress with them at:

Raoul Schonemann
(address supplied)

I'm sorry, but as you can probably gather from the beginning of this letter, I haven't been able to put much work in on your flute. As a matter of fact, I've only gotten the barrel assembly completed thus far. Doing woodwork here is a very slow process in itself as the only type of cutting tool we are allowed to possess are single-edge razor blades. Everything must be shaped with them or smaller tools we can fabricate from pieces of them (such as drills, scrapers, etc.).

At this point, though, I can tell you the following about your flute. It is of the Native American external channel format. I generally build this type for people who don't already play the flute as it doesn't require "educated lips" as does the transverse flute of the symphony orchestra. You simply blow gently into the mouthpiece to get it to speak. Your flute will be in the key of C# above middle C. This simply means that it will be pretty high pitched. I have chosen this key for two reasons. First, it keeps the overall length of the flute down to about 16." And, second, and most important, it's penetrating tone sounds great! I'll write with more info as I get further along with it.

In several of your letters you indicate that you would like for me to come and live in N. Wales should I be fortunate enough to get out of prison alive. And, from what I've learned of the country and its people, I can't think of anything I'd like better. Every photo I've ever seen of rural Wales literally resonates with a natural harmony so rare in our modern world. I truly think that I could be happy there. But let's be patient and see what God has in store for us.

Well, that about does it for this writing. I'd like to leave you with a story from my childhood. When I was five years old, I was introduced to a Japanese friend of my father's who also happened to be a Zen Master of some reputation. When the Master learned that I was interested in the Tao Te Ching at such a young age, he convinced my father to let me study with him. For my first lesson, the Master asked me to come to his house at four o'clock in the morning. When I arrived, he escorted me out into his small backyard garden in which there were a number of huge sunflowers. Placing a pillow on the ground in front of one of these sunflowers, he asked me to sit and pay particular attention to everything this flower did until he returned. I don't know how familiar you are with sunflowers, but at sundown the blooms close and droop down. At sunrise, the process is reversed, with the bloom rising to face the sun and reopening. I remember paying particular attention to each detail of this process as it occurred. And, when the Master returned, I must have taken thirty minutes recounting the process for him. He listened in polite silence. When I finished, he bent over to where his face was no more than six inches from mine, looked me in the eye, and asked, "Did it need your help?" I was so shocked by this question, that for a few seconds I couldn't even think. But in those few seconds, my whole perception of reality shifted and I became one with every-thing around me—the sunflower, the Master, the sky, everything. It is all truly one Entity! After I returned to my "normal" state, the Master explained what had

happened in terms I could understand. And
went on to tell me, from that day forward I
was to use that experience as a guide in
harmonizing myself with nature, which is
really God in disguise!

Take care and try not to worry too much
about me. For in the greater scheme of Life,
there are no unhappy endings!

That wonderful letter speaks for itself. From that time
on, the sunflower became our symbol. It later became our
death row symbol.

We did make contact with his lawyers, Raoul
Schonemann and Maurie Levin, and from that moment
on right until April of the following year, faxes were
flying between us across the Atlantic.

The next letter of 9 December 1997 was a very significant one:

Dear Joy:

Thank you for all of the beautiful cards
and letters. I feel terrible not having
answered each and every one of them. Unfortunately, attending to the details of my
appeal is monopolizing on my time right now.
However, after I am granted a stay I promise
to properly attend to my correspondence.

I sincerely wish I could give you some good
news about how things are going here. Unfortunately, it's still too early to say. I had
a rather lengthy visit with Raoul this past
Friday, during which we mapped out our
overall strategy. One of the things we plan
to do is contact the husband of the victim in

my case. He amazed the world at the time of the crime by telling the press that he did not want the death penalty for the perpetrators. And, on a number of occasions, he has voiced a willingness to meet with me in reconciliation. We are hoping that his voice will be heard by the board of pardons and paroles in our petition for clemency. Only time will tell.

Joy, I know you want to help me in any way you can and I think I have come up with a way in which you can have a real impact in my appeal and against the death penalty in general. As I told you when I asked you to become a witness to what was happening here in Texas, the state is relying on public apathy and a misinformation campaign to keep their killing machine going. However, if these people were made aware that the whole world was watching and they weren't fooling anyone, they would most likely stop the slaughter. So here is what I would like you to do. Ask anyone who is the least bit sympathetic to sit down and write a letter voicing their thoughts on the death penalty, and, if they feel so inclined, to request a reduction in sentence in my particular case. The letters should be sent to:

Texas Board of Pardons and Paroles
c/o Raoul D. Schonemann
(address supplied)

Margôt and I had been feeling so helpless. Now we were being asked to actually do something. We lost no time at all in contacting people all over the country, mounting what the press was to call a "campaign." These are just two of the letters that were sent:

23 December 1997

Dear Sirs,

Re: Mr. Lesley L Gosch—TDCJ-ID #000842 Ellis One, H-18, 2-7—Huntsville, Texas 77343

I have recently been approached about the case of Mr. Lesley Gosch, a prisoner on death row who is due to face execution on 15 January 1998.

Although I do not know the details concerning the case I have always been opposed to the enforcement of capital punishment and I appeal to you now on humanitarian grounds for clemency. As you may know, the Catholic Church has virtually ruled out the death penalty in its definitive Catechism. Although this is a subject of its teaching which it has developed and is still developing, the Pope's encyclical in 1995, *Evangelium Vitae*, marks a further stage in this development and I enclose a copy of the relevant paragraph from it.

I very much hope you will accede to this request.

With kind regards and best wishes.

Yours faithfully,
Basil Hume
Archbishop of Westminster

Archbishop's House
Westminster
London, SW1P 1OJ

3 January 1998

Dear Members of the Board,

I am writing on behalf of Mr. Lesley L. Gosch, who I believe has had a date set for his execution on January 15th next. I am well aware that the State of Texas still does enforce the death penalty for certain crimes, and I am not competent to comment on any of the details of Mr. Gosch's case. Nevertheless, I believe it is also the case that your Board has the power to waive the death penalty, and to commute it to some lesser sentence, and this is what I am sincerely asking you to consider, even at this late date.

My principal reason for asking you to reconsider is the evidence I have from those who know Mr. Gosch, and who are aware of the repentance and total conversion of heart which he has gone through during his lengthy period of incarceration. Since at least one of the principal motives underlying any penal sentence is the reform of the criminal, it seems to me to be unarguable that this aim has been fully achieved in Mr. Gosch's case, and that no further good purpose would be gained by carrying out the sentence.

I am, of course, aware that those who uphold the death penalty would wish also to stress the deterrent effect of maintaining this punishment as part of the legal system. But I suppose you are also well aware that the statistical evidence for the deterrent effect of the death penalty is, to say the least, very shaky indeed, as has been recognized in many countries and by many other States in the Union. You might therefore wish to consider whether the reputation of your own state for justice with mercy would be enhanced, rather than severely tarnished, by insisting upon that penalty in this case. The case has received considerable publicity in this country; and I am sure that any reconsideration of it would also be met with widespread approval over here, as well as elsewhere in the United States.

I therefore beg you to reconsider.

Yours sincerely,
Gerard J Hughes
Vice-Principal

Heythrop College
University of London

We learned later from Raoul, one of Lesley's lawyers, that a couple of hundred letters were received in support of Lesley's case and arguing against the death penalty. Many were from the Quaker community in the U.K. We had already seen on the Internet a powerful expression of the abolitionist view put out by the Friends in the U.S.A., and it felt good to have their support from this country. These letters were used by the lawyers to support the appeal case.

Lesley had been silent for a while but then this card came:

Joy:

I've been trying to get a letter off to you for 2 weeks, but it seems like every time I sit down to work on it, I get interrupted by something concerning this date! I've also had the worst case of flu I've had in years. Seems like when it rains, it pours!

Thank you
for everything!!!

```
P.S. Your flute is finished, tuned,
tested, and will be on its way to you the
very next time I see Raoul.
```

```
I've been in the Valley of the Shadow of
Death for so long I ought to be paying rent!
```

Both Lesley and Raoul had mentioned the possibility of a meeting between Lesley and Mr. Patton. At the time of the murder, Mr. Patton had expressed a desire for this. It had never happened, probably because there was no intermediary available to arrange it. It appeared that Mr. Patton was a reflective Christian and had declared himself against the death penalty. Raoul was now hoping to arrange such a meeting. This seemed to be a ray of hope which sent our spirits soaring.

Sadly, Mr. Patton was no longer interested. He had married again and, understandably, wanted to put all those sad events behind him. We had been pinning a lot of hope on this meeting so this was quite a blow. It seemed over and over again that by the world's standards, nothing could ever go right for Lesley. For the past four years he had been under the threat of death in this deadly cat-and-mouse game. That he had retained his balance, his humor, his hope and determination was nothing short of miraculous.

He even found time to send a reply to seven-year-old Joseph Wright, son of Michael Wright, enclosing a photograph of some of the flutes he was making:

```
Dear Joseph:
Thank you very much for your letter of
October 21st. I always enjoy hearing from
Sister Joy's friends. I'm sorry it's taken
```

me a while to answer your letter, but due to some recent events, I've been quite busy.

I assume from the number of instruments you play that you like music very much. I do too. Did you know that music is a kind of magic? It is. Music has the ability to change how we feel. Have you ever, when you were feeling down, played a recording of a piece of music you like a lot? What happened? I'd bet it wasn't very long before you started feeling better again. Well, science can't explain why this happens, so it can only be magic!

You say in your letter that you play the recorder. I do too. I also build various other types of flutes as a hobby. As a matter of fact, I'm working on one for Sister Joy right now. It's very similar in design to the flutes used by the American Indians. I'm sure she'll let you check it out when she gets it.

Well, that's all for now. Take care and keep practicing!

The date of 15 January 1998 grew ever closer. We were planning a vigil for the day itself. The sisters of my order in London were lighting a candle each evening and praying in the chapel. Many other friends around the country were also praying for Lesley.

On 13 January Margôt and I were at Saint Beuno's. After Mass a Jesuit friend, Michael Ivens, seriously ill, came up so very kindly to ask how we were. He held my hand in a truly compassionate way and said, "Would you like to come and celebrate Mass with me on January fifteenth?" We said that that would be wonderful.

We returned home to find a fax from Maurie Levin awaiting us. A stay had been denied, but she was exploring other avenues. It finished: "We spoke with Lesley yesterday evening and he sounded like he was on solid ground."

The vigil was to be held at our church at midnight. After making a few preparations in the morning we went over to Saint Beuno's for the Mass with Michael Ivens. We had been having a long spell of very grey, cloudy, and windy weather, and that day was no exception. We had a most beautiful and uplifting Mass together, just the three of us. Michael had been following Lesley's story very closely. Because of his own illness, he knew that he too was being gently stalked by death, but he was stunned at contemplating a man preparing to be killed at a determined hour—in what many regard as the most advanced country in the world. After the Mass, Michael reflected a little about God's attitude to those who have murdered. He highlighted the case of Cain and Abel and how God put a mark on Cain to *protect* him from the vengeance of his people. And that was way back in the Old Testament. Anyone familiar with the words of Jesus in the New Testament will find no justification for revenge of any sort. The previous day I had felt unable to eat, but after this beautiful experience we felt uplifted. We decided to go for lunch in the little village of Rhuddlan. As we drove there the clouds lifted and glorious shafts of light and sunshine broke through. We took this as a good omen and almost felt cheerful.

Back in Colwyn Bay, we went over to Saint Joseph's Church to make sure everything was in place for the vigil. We arranged the chairs in a circle with Lesley's photo in the center, surrounded by about one hundred candles. We wanted everything to be just right.

There were about twenty of us at the vigil. Our priest, another Michael, played soft music; we had readings and meditations and some appropriate songs. It was hard to believe that Lesley was now dead.

It was about 1:30 A.M. when John, Margôt and I arrived back at my house. The telephone rang. It was Colette Hume of the *Western Mail*: "Lesley is alive and back on death row!" We called Raoul and Maurie. They were, in their own words, "euphoric." The stay of execution had come from the Supreme Court, and apparently this was "most unusual." They said that in seven years of working on capital cases they had never achieved anything as good as this. What a roller-coaster of emotions we were embarked on. Maybe Lesley would not have to be killed, ever. Maybe his sentence *would* be commuted as we had all been requesting. We already knew that over two hundred letters had been sent from Wales and England to the Board of Pardons and Paroles and to Governor George Bush. It was tempting to think that all our letters had been effective.

Three days after the reprieve of 15 January, this letter came:

Dear Joy:

I got the most hilarious card from Sue Lusk yesterday in which she commented on my sense of humor. Yes, everyone says I have a "graveyard" sense of humor. To which I always reply is only appropriate for a person on death row! It's the humor in life that keeps it livable. A lot of funny things happen here. I'd like to share an incident with you which occurred a couple of weeks prior to my first execution date in 1992.

In this age of bureaucracy, nothing can happen in an institution like a prison without the accompanying ream of paperwork. And this is particularly true of something taken so seriously as an execution. One of the many forms which need to be completed in triplicate before the big event is called an "execution summary." It is a legal document recording the inmate's wishes concerning, among other things, the disposition of his body after the execution. This information is collected during an interview with the captain in charge of death row. In this particular case, a guy named West. He was sitting across his desk from me, big chew of tobacco in his jaw, when he asked me what I wanted done with my body. And, without missing a beat, I told him that I definitely wanted it resuscitated. This, shall we say unusual answer, caught the poor man so off guard that he swallowed his chew and turned as green as clover. Naturally, this took place in the midst of a gaggle of curious bystanders who immediately roared in laughter at seeing what had happened.

After the good captain regained his composure and browbeat his subordinates back into silence, he continued the interview by informing me that resuscitation was definitely not an option. To which I replied that I would have felt very stupid if St. Peter had informed me that it was . . . after my execution! This brought another round of laughter from the audience and ended the interview. I don't think the authorities ever did find out what I wanted done with my mortal remains. Just as well, a stay was granted and I got to keep them!

On a more serious note, I have been questioned by quite a number of people in the counseling business as to how I manage to stay so calm in the face of almost certain destruction. Much to their amazement, I tell them that it is simply because I have learned to live in the here and now. Let me explain. In the absence of actual physical pain, all of our miseries are created by the fantasies of our own mind. For example, a vivid fantasy of being murdered causes one nearly the same level of anxiety as the actual event. And this anxiety deteriorates our physical health as well. It's almost impossible to believe that we voluntarily do such a thing to ourselves, and on a daily basis, but we do. So how do we break out of this endless cycle? By simply disciplining ourselves to put 100% of our attention into whatever action we are involved in. The Buddhists call this practice "mindfulness." When you're walking, simply walk. Feel the rhythm of your body and the warm sun on your face. Don't try to imagine what's going to happen when you reach your destination, this will automatically take care of itself when you arrive! You have worked in a number of hospitals ministering to the terminally ill. How often have you heard these poor souls wonder where their life has gone. The horrible answer is that most of it has been frittered away on self-destructive fantasies. It really doesn't matter whether the fantasies bring pleasure or pain, they are keeping us from experiencing our lives. The reason I bring all of this up is the children which you come into contact with each day. They are still at an age when mindfulness is easy to learn and it only takes a minute to show them how. You cannot imagine the amount of suffering you will save the world.

As of this writing, there is still no news of a stay and I really don't expect one before Tuesday or Wednesday of next week. I say this because the last of the legal pleadings didn't get before the judge until the 8th. And, if for no other reason than the sheer volume of the documents, it's going to take the judge several days to review them and make a decision. And as the state is not opposing my habeas proceeding, I feel confident that a stay is forthcoming. However, only time will truly tell!

Well, thank you again for everything you and your countrymen have done for me. To repay that kindness has become my only reason for facing each new day. Take care and practice mindfulness!

```
   P.S. We rush through life, heeding little,
and soon we are only a memory of others. We
must  learn  to  love  each  moment,  as  a
connoisseur  savors  his  favorite  vintage.
For the grace of living is not what we do,
but  simply  being  alive!
```

This letter touched the hearts of many. On 17 January I received a written reflection from my godson, Michael Wright Junior, aged thirteen. On the evening of the fifteenth the whole family, all seven of them, had prayed together for Lesley at their London home. Afterward, Michael went upstairs and put his thoughts into words:

> On Thursday 15 January, Lesley Gosch, a man which common sense will tell you is an innocent and spiritual man, will be put to death, murdered by poison. The same system which condemns him and others as vile and sick humans then does the same thing as that which they condemn them for. I just don't understand it. This system is responsible for more murders than any human could commit. As Gandhi said: "An eye for an eye makes the whole world blind." What is the difference? A man is charged with murder and is murdered by the same people. It is a life and it causes more and more suffering. My heart is with Lesley, a wonderful man who seems to be innocent and will be in my eyes. He will be killed and for no reason. And what can a thirteen-year-old boy do that people won't ignore? God save Lesley!

In December 1998 Michael was confirmed with several other teenagers in the Church of the Sacred Heart, Kilburn, London. For his confirmation name, he chose "Lesley." It was a moving moment hearing the Bishop read out for all to hear: "Michael Lesley Wright, I confirm you. . ."

7

The Last Letters
from Lesley

After the wonderful news of the 15 January stay of execution, we were once more lulled into a false sense of security. This lasted until the following letter arrived on 9 February 1998:

Dear Joy:

Thank you so much for all of your wonderful cards and letters. They have played a great part in just keeping me going during these troubled times. Yes, I have recovered somewhat from my close encounter with the grim reaper, but it has become painfully obvious that one never really gets over such a thing. And it's not over yet! Yes, the U.S. Supreme Court has given me a stay of execution, but they have yet to agree to actually hear my case. Maurie tells me that the High Court will meet and officially decide this matter on February 20th. As you can probably guess, I'm on pins and needles until then. If the Supreme Court rules in my favor (agrees to hear my case), I still have a chance. If they don't, I'll receive another execution date and there will be nothing to stop it. So we're sitting in the eye of the hurricane right now. Your beautiful sunflower card of January 30th just arrived. I think that the book is a wonderful idea. However, let's see what happens on the 20th before we begin the project. If things don't go well, I might have to ghost write my chapter! Speaking of the flute, when I wrote earlier, I was under the impression that Maurie had mailed it to you. She hasn't. I found out last week. The mailing got held up so that photographs of the flute could be taken to show the Board of Pardons and Paroles. Fear not, it will be on its way shortly. I have just begun reading the most wonderful book. Its title is Voices of the First Day: Awakening in the Aboriginal Dreamtime. The book is a very thorough anthropology of the Australian Aborigines, but presented from the spiritual perspective. I have wondered for many years about these people's "Dreamtime." Is it in fact meditation? According to the book, it is, and a great volume of information is presented. Of course, from a practical point of view, they're human, I'm human, what else could it be?

Speaking of books, I just remembered that I am already featured in a book on death row. It was done about 5 or 6 years ago and it contains pictures of me here on the row. As a matter of fact, one of the photos featured in this book is on its way to you now! Should you want a copy of this book you need to contact the author/photographer.

Joy, there is someone I want you to contact here in the States. He is a close friend and can be of great help with your "Sunflower Campaign." Just call him, tell him what you're doing, and let things develop from there. I will even pay for the call. Just remember, coincidence is how God remains anonymous!!!

Well, I'm out of space. Thank you again for your love. Take care and be mindful!!!

A month later, this letter arrived:

Dear Joy:

For millennia the Chinese have passed their wisdom from generation to generation in the form of short stories. And over time, these stories have been compiled into larger works for ease of distribution and study. The following story is from one of the more popular compilations known as the Lieh-Tzu. Please give it multiple readings during your daily "quiet time." It will reveal a dimension of your psyche with which you are probably not real familiar.

THE MAN WHO GOT UPSET OVER NOTHING

"There was a man who was born in the country of Yen but grew up far away in the land of Ch'u. In his old age he had a longing for his homeland and decided to return there to live.

"As he journeyed toward his country of birth, he passed through the country of Chin. His companions on the road decided to play a trick on him. So one of them said, 'This is your hometown.' The man became silent and thoughtful.

"Another friend pointed to a building and said, 'Look, over there is your neighborhood temple.' The man sighed deeply.

"One companion led him to an abandoned house and said, 'Here's the home of your ancestors.' The poor man broke down in tears.

"Another companion motioned him toward a group of tombstones and said, 'Your ancestors are buried here.' The man began to weep loudly and bitterly.

"Seeing his distress, the friends decided the joke was over, so they told him they were just playing a trick on him.

"The homesick man was very embarrassed about his emotional outbursts and kept quiet for the rest of the way.

"When he finally reached his hometown and saw his ancestral house and the family tombs, he did not feel as bad.

"Can we say the man got upset over nothing when his friends teased him? We cannot say his emotions were false, because he truly believed what his friends told him. Our emotions are the result of our beliefs. They have nothing to do with what is really out there. If we believe one thing, then certain emotions will follow. If we believe some other thing, we will experience different emotions. Understanding this, the homesick man realized his emotions depended on what he believed he saw, not what was 'really' there. So, when he finally reached his homeland, he was less attached to his longing, and as a result his feelings were less stirred by his surroundings."

From: Lieh-Tzu: A Taoist Guide to Practical Living trans. Eva Wong

What the man in this story experienced is known in Eastern philosophy as maya, or illusion. By whatever name we call it, how many times a day do we fall victim to it? How many times a day do we get upset over nothing?

Then came the next blow. Raoul faxed us with the news that an execution date had been set for 23 March 1998. Kathryn Cox had told me that for a month after 15 January Lesley had been in a state of shock and that he had hardly been able to put a sentence together, "which was most unlike him." On the Friday before the March date was announced, he had just begun to be himself again. The new date was announced on the following Monday. The mind can only guess at what torment he was enduring.

On 1 March, I received this letter:

Dear Joy:

Thank you so much for all your cards and letters. They have contributed greatly to my peace of mind through all of my troubles. I sincerely wish that I could answer each and every one in detail, but to accomplish this task with my weak compositional skills the Lord would have to add several hours to each day. I am forwarding most of the clippings you send me to Kathy Cox. For some years she has been working on a book about the human side of death row and the articles broaden her database. She also has copies of all the writing for publication I've done during my stay here. Much of which details the lessons I've learned from the "catastrophes" which punctuate my life. And it is these same lessons which make me feel such a powerful bond with the supposedly primitive peoples of the world, like the Aborigines. For they too realize that God has a lesson to teach us in each and every detail of His creation, right down to how a rock or a stick lays on the ground. People have just gotten too busy thinking to pay attention to what's going on around them anymore. God is constantly appealing to us through the injured animal, the crying child, or even a beautiful sunset. And we stumble by, neither seeing nor hearing, trying to recall what we did with the grocery list. The real Bible is not a book, it's your life. And each day's awakening begins a new page.

Well, things here are still rather tense. For as of this writing, there is still no news of the Supreme Court's intentions concerning my case. Raoul was here yesterday for a visit and said that he was cautiously optimistic based on what little he could glean from his sources in the high court. This made me feel a little better as Raoul is usually quite pessimistic. Of course, who wouldn't be considering the state of the U.S. legal system. Raoul also told me during this visit that the Board of Pardons and Paroles had rejected my recent petition for clemency by a unanimous vote. This was not unexpected though, as the Board has yet to grant clemency to a capital defendant. Our only recourse at this point is to sue the Board and hope that we can accomplish what Karla Faye Tucker's attorneys couldn't—prove that the Board's practices are unconstitutional. Raoul feels that we have a strong case, especially with Karla Faye's useless death so fresh in the public's mind. It really disgusts me to have to use this poor lady's misfortune to try to save my own life, but it's the way the legal system works. And ultimately, it's not just my life that is at stake, it's everyone on death row. For they all come before the Board at some time in their journey through the legal system. Perhaps now is the time for the pendulum of judgement to reverse its swing.

As I believe I told you in a previous letter, I'm presently engrossed in a book on the Aborigines entitled Voices of the First Day: Awakening in the Aboriginal Dreamtime, by Robert Lawlor. I can't recommend this work highly enough to anyone who is sincerely seeking to draw closer to God. To give you some idea of why I feel like I do about the book, I would like to share one paragraph with you from the chapter I'm now studying.

"The teaching of compassion begins from the first moment an infant grabs some food or object and brings it to its mouth. The mother or any other relative, usually female, repeatedly uses these moments to plead with the child to share what it has with her. Of course, the mother never takes away what the child possesses or denies it anything it desires, but she finds many opportunities to pretend to be in great need of the infant's generosity. Reinforcing this constant dramatization by the mother is an open society in which people actively share everything with each other. Whenever a weak, ill, or harmless person or creature passes the child's path, the mother fusses

over it and showers it with attention, even
if it is a scraggly lizard: 'Poor thing,' the
mother declares with great, heartfelt
emotion. Food is never denied to anyone or
any creature that is hungry. The child experiences a world in which compassion and pity
are dramatically directed toward the temporarily less fortunate. The constant
maternal dramatization of compassion in the
early years orients a child's emotions
toward empathy, support, warmth, and generosity."

The reasons I chose this particular passage
are manifold. First, it proffers considerable evidence to support my belief that the
Europeans have destroyed vastly superior
cultures wherever they went to colonize. My
second reason involves you as a teacher. I
know very little about the training girls get
concerning raising children in our modern society. But I can't help but suspect that they
are based upon the "survival of the fittest"
philosophy much more often than they are compassion. Is there any way in which this simple
technique employed by Aboriginal mothers to
teach their children compassion, be inte-
grated into the training girls from the "advanced" countries receive? Or is this already
the situation? I can't help but believe, that
if this simple paradigm were adopted, that
many of our social ills might start clearing
up within a few generations. Isn't it worth a
try?

Also, in your last letter you mentioned that you too might like to read Voices of the First Day. I think this would be great as we could compare our feeling on various aspects of Aboriginal society. To this end I am enclosing info on a distributor of the book in England:

Deep Books Ltd.
(address supplied)

Joy, in a previous letter you asked me to tell you about my life. I have always been reluctant to do so because my life really hasn't been very pleasant. Take, for example, my birth. I am what is referred to in polite circles as a "love child." That is, I am the product of an unwed teenager's accidental pregnancy. Both my father and mother were barely seventeen years old when I was born and neither was emotionally prepared to deal with an infant. But they tried to make a go of it anyway. And everything went pretty well for the first eighteen months. Then my father, Ronald Tontz, was killed in a grisly auto accident. I gave his name here so you would recognize him in one of the photos I sent you. My mother, bless her heart, tried to carry on by herself but just couldn't cope. To put it in her own words, "I knew it was time to put him up for adoption when I caught myself twisting his leg off because he wouldn't stop crying."

Forty years later the damage to that leg still gives me fits. But I don't hold it against her because I know from my own experience how hard life can be. My paternal grandparents adopted me shortly after this incident and a new chapter in my life began. The telling of which I shall save for my next letter.

I received a Sunday Missal in the mail several days ago. Quite a beautiful edition too. Unfortunately, no paperwork arrived with it so I don't know who to thank for it. While searching for clues to the identity of my benefactor, I discovered that the texts in this edition are approved for Wales. Did you or Margot send it? If so, thank you very much! Of course, now I'll have to start going to Mass again so I can use it.

As I was finishing up this last paragraph, your letter of February the 14th arrived. And the stationery on which it is written is very beautifully designed. As a matter of fact, if my memory serves me correctly, the sunflower on the stationery looks almost exactly like that sunflower did in my Zen master's garden so long ago. Thank you for reviving and clarifying this memory.

I was very, very pleased to hear that you have been in contact with Russell Perkins. For I cannot speak highly enough of the man. He has been my teacher, friend and inspiration during some very dark hours. But I think most important, Russell was instru-

mental in my discovering the Christ as He
incarnated for our generation. For there has
never been a time when the Christ was not
present on the Earth.

Well, I was just handed a stack of legal
documents which I need to study and forward
to Maurie and Raoul in this evening's mail,
so I best get on it. I would like to take this
opportunity to again thank you and your
friends for everything you've done in my
behalf. For I am aware that I am still here
through no merit of my own, but only the
prayers of kind folks like yourself. Take
care and be mindful!

P.S.: True patience means having absolute
confidence in God.

The date of 24 March came, and we waited with bated
breath. We hardly dared hold another public vigil so we
just prayed quietly at home, knowing there was very little
chance of his surviving this one. Eventually a call came
through: the lawyers had won a stay on a technicality.
Two cards arrived from Lesley:

Adequate words do not exist to express my
appreciation for all of the love and support
which you and your countrymen have shown me
in my darkest hour. I am certain that my life
was spared because of no merits on my part,
but the prayers of you and your friends!

And:

Dear Joy:

I just received the postcard showing Colwyn Bay and Rhos-on-Sea. Now I understand your reluctance to be away from home. Where you live gives new meaning to the word "beautiful." Yes, I would like nothing better than to see you again. And the 21st & 22nd would be perfect. You are still on my visitors list, but I'll need to add Margot. Please send me her full name, address, age, etc., ASAP, so I can add her to my list.

The universe is the manifest portion of the being we call "God." So the universe is within God and God is within the universe—and us. "The Kingdom of Heaven is within you." The purpose of a human life is to enter this kingdom before physical death. How? By renewing your mind. The human mind has two positions: looking outward at the world through the senses, and looking inward at itself and the Kingdom of Heaven beyond. Only our thoughts obscure the kingdom and only our thoughts create our "self" or personality. By constantly looking within, we silence the mind, crucify the "self," and enter the Kingdom of Heaven. This is the essence of meditation and what Paul meant when he said, "I die daily." So do I.

On 10 April I received Lesley's final letter: he knew it would happen this time. He was as well prepared as anyone could be:

Kindness is the highest wisdom!

Dear Joy:

Thank you so much for all of your wonderful cards and letters. They are a great solace in my time of troubles.

I have just been given your loving letter of March 19th and noted its contents. It was very pleasing to hear that you are now in contact with Russell & Judith Perkins. They are both very devoted to God. Yes, Russell & Judith were here last week for a visit. Unfortunately, the same thing happened which happened with your visit. I was unexpectedly bench-warranted back to San Antonio the day before they arrived in Huntsville. And, naturally, I didn't get back to the prison until several days after they had returned home. I would imagine that they're quite upset with me over this little fiasco, but I really had no way of warning them not to come. I am planning to write them a rather lengthy letter of explanation and apology in the next couple of days.

My trip to San Antonio was positively awful. The journey itself is about 4 hours in duration, nonstop. So water or a rest room break is out. I spent about the last 90 minutes of the trip back in excruciating pain thanks to this practice. And what adds insult to injury here is the fact that it was all completely unnecessary. The entire business of issuing me a new execution date (April 24th) could have been conducted by mail. Unfortunately, the presiding judge is an elected official and feels that he must impress the voters with his efficiency at dispensing justice. What a joke! The only good thing to come from this entire ordeal was the progress I made during my meditations.

Joy, I don't know of a way of telling you this that isn't going to be painful, but barring a genuine miracle, this April 24th execution is most likely going to take place. My appeals are exhausted. Raoul & Maurie have some ideas concerning new issues, but they are all very long shots. How do I feel about dying? Well, I don't want to die any more than anyone else does, but I came to grips with the fact that it's inevitable a long time ago. This is why I work so hard at living every moment as God gives them to me. They're all we have! Sitting around worrying about some moment in the future which I may or may not have is insane. And worse, all of these ruminations rob me of this very moment. I guess what I'm trying to say is that I'll deal with death when it comes. Because to worry about it before then is to die a million times before you take your last breath. Anyway, God would never have us die if it wasn't good for us!

I was helping my neighbor find a passage in the Bible this morning when I came across Matthew 26:39, the prayer of Jesus at Gethsemane. All of my life, I have been told by Sunday school teachers, etc., that when

Jesus here asks that "the cup pass from Him," He is demonstrating the human side of the God-man by asking His life be spared. I beg to disagree. For folks that look at His words in this way are only projecting their own inability to love their enemies on Jesus. They don't realize that when Jesus asks that "the cup pass from Him," He's not asking for Himself, but for those who are about to murder Him. For Jesus is aware of the condemnation they are about to call down upon their heads by crucifying Him. And He is trying to save them from this condemnation by asking the Father to institute another course of action. Also, Jesus continues praying for His murderers from the cross: "Forgive them, Father, for they know not what they do." If I were to have a "last wish" it would be to have the strength to follow His lead and forgive my murderers from the death chamber.

Well, that's all I can think of for now. I'll write again in a few days, maybe I'll have some better news. Take care and live in the moment.

P.S.: "God is dead."—Nietzsche
"Nietzsche is dead."—God

I showed this letter to Margôt; we looked at each other, the enormity of it sinking in. This time it was Margôt who said to me, "Joy, I think we have to go. You have to be there for him."

"I think you are right," I replied.

We gave ourselves the weekend to reflect and pray about it. By the Monday, we both knew we had to go. As before, once the decision had been made, we lost no time in setting it all in motion, including fixing up our visiting hours with Lesley and Ted. In that part of the preparation, Sue Lusk, our Texas Human Writes co-ordinator, was a tremendous help. And Sr. Mary Dumbrill offered to come from London to look after my cat. She did it most willingly, making her retreat and praying for us all.

8

The Second Visit to Texas

When we had been preparing for our first Texas visit, there had been considerable excitement and apprehension. Excitement, for me at least, in visiting the U.S.A. for the first time. The sheer distance to Texas was awe-inspiring. There was also apprehension of going specifically to a place of killing: America's home-grown "killing field," to visit a dear friend who was in imminent danger of being executed. Apart from this aspect, Texas was a totally unknown quantity.

This second time it was all rather different. We knew the ropes, so to speak. Somehow I felt unbelievably calm about facing the trip. We were going out there for Lesley's inevitable death and that was a sobering thought. We planned to change planes at Gatwick this time, rather than Paris.

A few days before we were due to leave, our good friend Ceidiog Hughes of HTV decided that he would come with us. Every Wednesday afternoon at Huntsville's death row is "media day." Ceidiog had spoken about the possibility of this some weeks before, yet it would be such an unusual thing for him to do that I don't think he really thought it would actually happen. We were delighted as it meant that probably we would have Lesley on tape forever. But, above all, it would give the much needed publicity to what goes on in Huntsville. It was a last-minute decision, and Ceidiog was scheduled to take a plane just a few hours after ours. His program would tell the whole of Wales and beyond what was happening in Texas.

Our flights were uneventful apart from a minor thunderstorm—which I always find a little scary. As we prepared to land at Houston, we must have been the closest the pilot could possibly get to actually landing when he started to climb upward again. Apparently this happens quite frequently at major airports: there is no space to land and the pilot has no option but to go up and out for a while before making a second attempt. We were up for about half-an-hour. We finally landed safely at 2:00 P.M.

Ceidiog was due to arrive at 5:00 P.M. Should we wait to welcome him or head for Huntsville? Since he was going to be based in Houston, we decided to go straight on. A cab took us to our car rental company and soon, once more, we were on the way to Hospitality House. Again, the gigantic statue of Sam Houston was there on the horizon to greet us. And suddenly—there we were at 912 Tenth Street, driving up to Hospitality House. *That* felt good. And sure enough, there was Bob, ever kindly Bob, to welcome us. Some young Italians were immediately picking up our bags. Oh yes, this place feels like home! It's an amazing community of love, sharing and friendship. There were in fact nine young Italian men and women who had come over to visit prisoners they had been befriending: one prisoner, Jo Cannon, was scheduled for execution two days before Lesley. The Italians were an incredibly warm, compassionate, friendly group and it was a joy meeting them. That is one of the benefits of staying at Hospitality House—you never know who you are going to meet up with.

By this time we were pretty tired, having been on the move for the past twenty-three hours. The following day we had to be up bright and early to begin our visits to Ellis One. Thank God for Margôt: for her wonderful companionship, for her driving skills, and her excellent sense of direction. After a welcome cup of tea and passing the iron over a few clothes, we set off for downtown Huntsville and our favorite haunt: the Golden Corral! In Texas our brains constantly move in top gear. Every moment is precious; no opportunity must be lost. On our first evening at the Golden Corral two young waiters, Sam and Danny, commented on our English accents (always a great conversation starter) and of course we told them why we were there. We got the usual "Wow!" response. They were fairly and squarely for the death penalty, and gave us the usual reasons. For good measure, they told us about a young guy they knew who, courtesy of America's "three strike" policy, had just been given a life sentence for stealing a box of matches.

Sam and Danny were in fact students at the Sam Houston University in Huntsville, working evenings at the Golden Corral. We ended up having a fairly in-depth conversation and, as so often happens, their views became less black and white as they slowed down a bit and considered other ways of looking at the crime and punishment issue. They welcomed us to return, and by the time we had all finished they had given us names and phone numbers of anti-death-penalty contacts at the university, including that of Denis Longmire, a professor of criminology who, we later learned, attends all of the execution vigils. For all our negative feelings about Texas, it has to be said that people there are second to none in friendliness and openness. We liked Sam and Danny a lot, and we did indeed return to the Golden Corral and talked some more with them. Thanks to them, we arranged a meeting at the university chaplaincy.

Back at Hospitality House we discovered there had been a telephone call for us; it was Ceidiog calling from Houston. He called back later. Like us, he was very tired after the flight. He was somewhat dazed at being in America for the first time and apprehensive about the task that lay ahead of him. And as if that weren't enough, he learned on arrival that his mother, who suffers from cancer, had been rushed into hospital. Having been in situations like that myself, I really felt for him. We urged him to have a meal and to try and get some rest.

The next day Ceidiog told us he hadn't slept all night. Today he had to meet up with Marcus, the photographer who was going to work with him. Marcus lived in Houston and would drive Ceidiog over to Huntsville. Ceidiog had found that so many thoughts were going around in his head. We were exactly the same: throughout the night, sleeping a little and waking a lot. We are always awake early. During the night, the air-conditioning is on constantly, and as on death row there is rarely total silence. But there the comparison ends; Hospitality House really is a very special place.

We were up at 6:00 A.M. By 8:15 we were driving into the parking lot at Ellis One, death row. The fifteen-mile trip is a pleasant one. The countryside was quite beautiful at this time of year, and the fields were covered with spring flowers. Texas is famous for one particular flower:

the gorgeous bluebonnet. The season for them had almost passed, but a few remained.

Approaching the prison, you begin to see figures in white moving about in trucks or already working in the fields. These are the "Population" prisoners starting their day's work, watched over by the inevitable guards, several on horseback, their rifles, as ever, close at hand. One could only think back to the days of slavery; most of the figures in white are black men. On the way too we pass the very shabby houses of the poor, mostly black families: little more than shacks. What a history of sorrow and suffering.

Margôt, having visited Ellis One on our previous visit, was familiar with the routine: no lingering at the parking lot. Straight to the hut near the entrance. Wait to be acknowledged. Show your ID. Wait until told to proceed. Proceed. Walk through the iron bars which will be opened electronically by the women guards in the high tower above. Then through another identical set of bars. Walk straight on. Be composed. Don't show any feelings. Now walk through the doors into Ellis One itself. Don't be surprised at the highly polished floor, the civilized appearance. Texas is proud of its prisons. Look how clean everything is. Go to reception. Show ID again. Leave car keys, bags, ID. Take nothing with you but a small amount of money to buy drinks and snacks for your friend. (We are grateful for that concession.) Wait to be called.

"Margôt Aczel to twenty-nine." "Joy Elder to eighteen." We are on our way.

Here at last, six months on, I was walking into my visiting place on death row. Today was Tuesday. Tomorrow Jo Cannon was to be executed and, on Friday, Lesley. His close friends from New Hampshire, with whom I had been in contact, were due to arrive that evening, and also a couple from Houston. Normally Lesley had no visitors at all apart from Kathryn Cox, his spiritual adviser and respected friend. Now there were six of us to be scattered throughout the days and hours ahead. Not only that, he had all his friends on Ellis One to say goodbye to; he had the last of his property to dispose of and, above all, he somehow had to make his final preparations for leaving this world behind and moving on to meet his God. This would be his third visit to the death house to face his killing. There was hardly even the slightest chance that this time he would be reprieved. He had given away all his art materials several weeks before. He explained to me later that if a prisoner hasn't disposed of absolutely everything, it is simply "trashed" by the guards.

The death row visiting hall is a large rectangular room divided lengthways into two parts. Down one side are the prisoners on lockdown; they are the ones whose executions are drawing near. A prisoner with an execution date is sent to lockdown for a month before his date. Lesley had spent three separate months on lockdown before each of his scheduled executions, not counting the times he had been bench-warranted to San Antonio. It is not a pleasant experience. These prisoners are segregated from all their friends and are no longer allowed to participate in the work program. They are allowed out of their cells for just one hour. This happens early in the morning when it's very cold, so Lesley didn't usually bother. They are still allowed to write letters and receive mail and to read.

On the other side of this division in the visiting room are the other prisoners who, if they are on the work program, have the privilege of walking freely to the visiting booth, while those on lockdown are always brought along in handcuffs. On lockdown, as well as those awaiting execution, are those who are not on the work program, either because they choose not to be or because their behavior does not qualify them for working. Unlike the others, for some obscure reason, the ones on lockdown are placed in cages. The reasons for most things on death row are obscure. It is all so dreadfully humiliating, and while you are outwardly behaving quite naturally and normally toward the men you see in the cages, inwardly you are cringing for them and you feel hurt by this.

As I walk down to my booth I see that Kathryn Cox is already sitting there and I'm delighted to see her. We had missed the chance of meeting last time, and I really wanted to get to know her as I had heard so much about her from Lesley. He too had been very keen for us to meet.

For an hour we were a threesome and, despite everything, it was really enjoyable. Kathryn is a most remarkable lady: seventy-three years old and as pretty as a picture with a lovely bubbly nature. A member of the Salvation Army, she has been a pastor for fifty years, the last fifteen of which she has been ministering on death row. She also has twenty-one thousand prison students enrolled in her Bible courses. What a dynamic woman. She wore navy trousers and a very attractive, multicolored blouse. The prisoners love to see bright colors; it really cheers them up in those depressing surroundings where all the prisoners wear white and the guards wear grey. Kathryn lives at Dallas, 180 miles away, but at least twice a week she drives down to Huntsville. On those days she is up at 3:00 A.M., breakfasting at McDonald's in downtown Huntsville by 6:00 A.M. She tells me she rarely gets to bed before 1:00 A.M. I can certainly see why Lesley has been inspired by her.

After an hour Kathryn leaves, and Lesley and I have almost three hours together. He tells me how tired he is. We talk about it and about what is happening, about what the lawyers are doing, about his life as it is at the moment, on lockdown. He is anxious to know about our journey, if we had good flights, and so on. He asks me to thank Margôt for the *Daily Missal* she had sent him. He passed it on to Cliff, a devout Catholic, who has since been executed (11 June 1998). I hear that the missal is to be sent across the Atlantic once more, this time to Sue Lusk, our Texas Human Writes co-ordinator. So impressed was she by Cliff's faith, that she wants to explore the faith herself.

Lesley talks to me about the flute he made for me, and says he's sorry that I haven't yet received it. His lawyers had promised to mail it to me—he supposes they have forgotten or haven't had time.

The time flew by and it was so good to have been able to talk with Lesley in physical conditions that were a great improvement on those in San Antonio. Four previous visiting hours gone. I could not see him the next day. It would be four hours again on Thursday and then a couple of hours on the dreaded Friday.

We said goodbye, and as I walked away I saw that a lady was walking toward me with the saddest face I had ever seen, her eyes full of tears. I guessed who she was: Jo Cannon's mother. "Are you Jo's mother?" I asked gently. She looked at me and put her arms around me. As we embraced, I found myself weeping with her. It was bad enough for me knowing that Lesley was going to be killed, but what can it be like for the *mother* of a death-penalty victim?

She told me Jo's story. At four years old he was knocked down by a car which left him with multiple brain injuries, as a result of which he became hyperactive and difficult to cope with. She was constantly asking for help for him, but never got it. As a teenager he became more and more difficult to handle. In his innocence he would break into neighbors' houses and steal things—for example, pieces of chicken which he would then sit outside and eat. The result of this was that he would be picked up by the police and be thrown into the county jail for a while. Way out of control, he was taken in by a lawyer's wife who felt inspired to care for him. One evening, aged sixteen, he got drunk and killed her. He was put on death row at nineteen, in 1979, after three years in county jails.

Now, after nineteen years on death row, he was about to be executed for a deed that he couldn't even remember. Jo had become completely institutionalized and, ironically, the stability and routinized way of life had the calming effect on him that should have been made possible for him all those years ago. Completely peaceful and harmless as he was, he had to die. They needed the spaces on death row. For every one being killed, four new people are brought in—mainly in their twenties, though some are younger.

Jo's mother introduced me to her son. He gave me a big smile.

During that week we saw a lot more of Jo's mother and his sister, Bernie, as they too were staying for the whole week at Hospitality House. Later on in the week, Bernie's husband joined them and we would all sit and chat in the evenings. Bernie's husband told us that when the guards are being trained they are told not to get close to prisoners. They are to imagine that every prisoner had raped their mother.

During the rest of Tuesday we had a bit of a rest, went to visit the malls, and to eat at a Chinese restaurant we had visited the year before. We found the same Malaysian waitress who we had talked with then. She remembered us, and we heard all the news of her family and she heard about our second visit to death row.

When we arrived back at Hospitality House, the Italians were there with Mrs. Cannon and Bernie. The atmosphere was full of deep sadness. Pastor Bob had told us it was going to be a hard week for all at Hospitality House, with families and friends of two executees staying. It was indeed a hard week. A week like no other. Where in the world could you experience things like this? In Iraq, Iran or China maybe. But in the Western world? It seems so inconceivable.

There was a totally surreal feel to the events of that week. You would sit, move, walk to the chapel or whatever—always conscious of practicing extreme tact and at the same time sharing deep love and empathy. Tears were never far from the surface. Thankfully, one of the rules at Hospitality House is that it's lights out at 10:00 P.M.—which simply means you leave the lounge at that time. You are always free to go and get a drink or a snack. Everything is thought out very carefully so as to give you the maximum help and comfort. Shampoo, hair dryers, toothpaste—all are available for you if you need them.

As usual, we slept in fits and starts. How can you rest easy when the next day a man will be killed? Yes, Jo Cannon killed someone all those years ago, and any death by killing is a truly dreadful thing. But Jo, with his brain damage, nineteen years later, was in reality an innocent. In the system that kills people methodically, clinically, there is no innocence. Only a dire guilt. I long for more people of Texas to stop and reflect, truly reflect on what they are doing. Then perhaps the sparks of revulsion would ignite a fire that would bring more compassion into the world of crime and punishment.

On Wednesday morning we hardly dared look at Mrs. Cannon and Bernie. At times like this you truly need God's help, the loving gifts of the Spirit of Wisdom, to walk side by side with family members about to lose a loved one by execution.

We set off as usual to arrive for 8:00 A.M. Ted, Margôt's friend, had put me on his visiting list, which delighted me as I knew Lesley would be pleased. After all, he had "given" Ted to Margôt in the first place and he and Ted were good friends. I had heard so much about Ted from Margôt and it would be good to meet him. When I did, what struck me was the light that shone from his clear grey eyes. His voice was soft and gentle, his smile transparent. Ted had been received into the Church at Easter. Like Lesley, he had spent eleven years on death row: years that had been spent studying and entering deeply into the essential questions of life: Who am I? Why am I here? What is life for? Who is God? What is God's relationship to me? Is there an afterlife? Lesley ultimately found most of his answers in Eastern mysticism; Ted found his in the Catholic Christian faith.

I was deeply impressed by Ted's graciousness, his sheer giftedness in the Lord. Time and our death row friends just move you as nothing or no one else could.

Margôt left us alone for a while and Ted explained to me exactly how the situation was regarding Catholic chaplains on death row. Until about two years ago there had been a most wonderful one, a certain Richard (deacon) Lopez, but he had since been appointed to chaplaincy administration. He was desperately missed by all, and the current situation left much to be desired.

The good news concerned a certain Fr. James Walsh, a Franciscan, who came every month from Boston to spend a few days ministering to the Catholics. It was through the pastoral care of Richard and James that Ted, Garry and Cliff had been drawn to the Church. And what fervent Christians they were. They put us to shame!

As Ted talked, I was wondering to myself about the chaplaincy situation, as Margôt had mentioned this problem several times before. Hearing Ted talk it was easier to get a picture of what was going on and who the different characters in the chaplaincy scenario actually were.

The time with Ted whizzed by. He had in the course of it told me that his cell-mate, Garry, had also put me on his visiting list and that he wanted me to write to him. So, just as I was about to lose Lesley, I would gain Garry.

I moved down to the booth where Garry was waiting for me. I was greeted with a big smile—Garry is a great smiler. After the introductions and a bit of chit-chat, he looked at me and said, "I suppose you know why I'm here?" I replied that I didn't know, and then I remained silent, hoping he would tell me. If death row prisoners choose to tell you this, they are indeed showing you a great deal of trust. It also helps you in that you know more of the person's story.

Garry was so open, so honest. He told me of his crime, and I was deeply moved, partly because of his frankness—but most of all because I felt this rush of awareness of what forgiveness is. What God's love is. Here was a young man who had done a dreadful deed who had turned to God and for ten years had been seeking God and—like Ted—had been doing penance willingly. I found myself thinking how God loves such people, how dear they are to him; and at this moment, Garry in particular. At the time of the crime, like so many others, Garry was drunk and remembers very little about it.

I had heard from Ted that Garry believed that God had forgiven him, but he could not forgive himself. That is the cross that Garry and others like him on death row have to carry daily. Alongside that, of course, is the knowledge that you too will be killed: this year, next year, sometime. Not "never." Sometime. How do they keep sane bearing these dreadful burdens? The answer is that some don't; they simply go completely mad. Others sleep all the time. Ted, Garry and Cliff did all in their power to come to terms with all of their heavy baggage. The result is a glorious testament to the power and the loving mercy of God.

"People always turn their lives around on death row," say the cynics. Not true. Some do—genuinely. Some don't. "They are monsters," others say. This is definitely not true. The unconverted may be mad or wild, but they are not monsters. They are lost, terrified, lonely, bewildered, mentally ill. Many should be hospitalized.

After settling down into our visit I found Garry to be a genuine, humble, very normal thirty-year-old, though he admitted he had become institutionalized, and that he would now find it very hard to live outside prison. I already knew a bit about Garry via Ted, via Margôt. Ted had originally told us that Garry had no penfriends, and so I'd been able to find him a couple of excellent ones: Charlotte and Nadia, who were students. I was honored that he wanted me as his penfriend too. Being so religious, I think the idea of writing to "Sister" Joy appealed to him! Before we left, he gave me (courtesy of a guard) an exquisite rosary he had made for me. Ted had given me a beautiful box. They ask so little and yet give all they have to give: the fruit of their love, the work of their hands. They would definitely smile at us in disbelief if we said this, but we feel they are our saints. Visiting death row turns all your preconceived notions upside down.

We usually left the prison in a fairly subdued mood. There was always so much to think about as we walked down the hall and through all the checkpoints out to the parking lot. It was good to feel the warm sun again. For the past four hours we had been totally focused on Ted and Garry, oblivious to the world outside.

Now there were two matters immediately presenting themselves: the conversation about chaplains, and the fact that six hours from now Jo Cannon would be killed. Regarding the chaplaincy situation, we decided we must pray about it. For Jo, we would be present outside The Walls prison at 5:30 P.M. to take part in the vigil and protest.

We drove yet again through the avenues of wild flowers. We saw the men in white working silently in the fields. If someone were unaware that death row was just behind them, they could believe they were in the grounds of a huge monastery. Everywhere around the prison is neat and trim. Some prisoners were tending little rose gardens. The physical environment is probably far superior to that of many prisons in other parts of the world, and you have to keep reminding yourself of what is taking place within. Today it was Jo Cannon's turn. On Friday, it would be Lesley's turn. No wonder we were subdued.

By now the heat is becoming quite intense so we head for our soda parlor and have a cool drink. At 3:00 P.M. I have to be at Hospitality House for a briefing about

Lesley's forthcoming killing. This briefing is to be given by the two official prison chaplains. They are paid by the prison and are part of the establishment. I'm not at all looking forward to this briefing session. Margôt drives me home to prepare for it while she returns to Huntsville to buy felt-tip pens and sheets of cardboard to make some posters for the vigil.

The two prison chaplains arrive for the briefing. Present are Kathryn Cox, the couple from Houston, and Russell and Judith Perkins from New Hampshire, all people of peace. The two couples belong to the Eastern sect that Lesley is part of. Russell is a Harvard graduate and is now a teacher. One of the chaplains is an attractively dressed woman. I have never heard any of the prisoners mentioning these chaplains. Their being part of such a prison system makes me instinctively wary of them.

During the briefing they explain to us the exact process by which Lesley will be killed: first, he will be given a shot to "put him out." This is like the one you get before major surgery. Secondly, there will be a shot to implode the lungs. Thirdly, a shot to stop the heart.

We are told that we mustn't become emotional or make any loud noise. We must breathe deeply in case we faint. It is sickening. "You still have time to change your minds," says the male chaplain. I make no comment and neither do any of the others. I just want them to go away. I am meant to appreciate that this is a service laid on for our benefit in order to help us cope with the execution. It is all so gross. This is the life of Lesley Gosch. Lesley the peaceable one. Lesley the scholar. Lesley the mystic, the artist, the engineer, the speaker of five languages. Lesley the good Samaritan within and without the walls of Ellis One.

Finally, they leave. We all quietly go our own ways, one in mind and heart, united in a place beyond words.

At 4:00 P.M. Margôt is here and we make our posters. At 5:30 we are down at The Walls. Emotionally my thoughts are with Lesley, but we have to be here for Jo too. We get out of our car and walk along a grass verge to stretch our legs a bit. Two young guards come up to us and ask who we are and what we are doing. We tell them we have come from Wales to protest at the executions. They pass on. Margôt is sure they have been sent by a higher authority to check on us.

Jo Cannon's sister and other family members are his witnesses. His mother could not bear to watch her son being killed so she is outside The Walls, not so far from us. Six o'clock strikes. As usual, we all go quiet. Time passes . . . 6:30 . . . 7:00 P.M. What is happening? Margôt and I are due to visit the university chaplaincy at 7:00 P.M. to share our thoughts on the death penalty with a group of students.

It gets very hot standing in the sun. Hot like Africa. Memories. I was once nearly imprisoned myself in Tanzania. We move a short distance away to the shade of some trees. Suddenly an ambulance comes screaming around a corner and heading for the crowd at the walls. It stops. The next thing we see is a guard pushing people out of the way and shouting: "Can't you see, we're trying to save this woman's life!" It was Mrs. Cannon. She had fainted and was being rushed to hospital.

Jo should surely be dead by now. So why are we not hearing anything, nor seeing both sets of families being led away in the customary fashion? The situation does not feel right at all.

Finally, at 7:30 P.M. it filtered through that Jo was dead. There had been some "difficulties" with his execution, and later we heard the details. Jo had been strapped to the gurney in the usual manner, but then the machine wasn't working so he had to be taken off the gurney to wait until it was functional again. On to the gurney again. Unbelievably, there was a second hitch. The veins in his arms collapsed. It was 7:30 P.M. by the time Jo was pronounced dead: for a murder he committed twenty-two years ago. His killing had taken an hour longer than the norm.

Bernie and her mother were back at Hospitality House that same evening. Mrs. Cannon looked as if she'd aged a good twenty years. Bernie was doing a good job of comforting her. Mrs. Cannon was given high doses of Valium and slept for twenty-four hours. Jesus, have pity on all bereaved mothers, especially those who have been bereaved in such a terrible way. The newspaper headlines the next day read "Jo Cannon's execution goes ahead in unusual circumstances."

By the time we arrived at the university chaplaincy we were an hour late, and only three students were left. We spoke with them for a while, and then we left for the Golden Corral where we enjoyed the company of Danny and Sam—whose attitudes to the death penalty were softening by the minute. And finally home to bed.

Thursday. The last full visit with Lesley. Margôt had used up all her visiting time with Ted so she drove me to Ellis One and said she would pick me up later. Now it was my turn to be alone on death row.

It was sad, so sad, seeing Jo Cannon's booth now empty. His mother, instead of sitting there with him, was sleeping her pain away, oblivion being the only way to ease it.

Lesley's booth was empty, as were several others. I chatted with a family in the next booth. They were friends of the person they were waiting for. There was a little girl aged five. She had made a colorful card for the prisoner; "She is a very caring child," her mother told me. In another booth sat a young black man looking very tense as he discussed his case with two lawyers, a male and a female. Another life hanging in the balance, and almost surely headed in the one deadly direction.

And then came Lesley. I hadn't seen him since Tuesday and today, Thursday, he seemed almost bright. He told me he had slept well the night before. Our booth was at the very end of the hall, next to a wall that was in the process of being knocked down.

For two-thirds of our visit we were subjected to loud drilling and knocking. In these intense situations the only way to cope is to try and ignore all the obstacles and get on with what is important. Somehow, in spite of the noise, it was a wonderful visit.

We spoke briefly about the latest news from the lawyers—which looked far from hopeful—and then we spoke about other things. He told me how he would love to live in a cottage in rural Wales where he could paint, work and meditate. If not Wales, Costa Rica.

He told me about his wife, a Mexican girl from a well-to-do family, how they lived in a beautiful house belonging to her family in Mexico, how the authorities had come after him there for his involvement in the revolution in Nicaragua. Luckily, his mother-in-law had foiled them by saying he was out and would be back by 10:00 P.M. When they returned, a family member who was the governor of the region was ready for them. He sent them packing on the next plane back to Texas. (Margôt and I have our own theory that *this* is why they "got him" in the end.) He told me how he and his young wife, at her request, had been on a trip to Paris.

We talked about books and music. He spoke of his special love for folk music, the music of the people. Every Thursday evening he listened to a folk music program from Edinburgh.

He also invited me to talk about myself and my life. On the one hand, it felt a bit selfish to do that. How could I be even thinking about myself, still less talking about myself, when the next day Lesley would be strapped down and killed? On the other hand, this was the day when we were truly sharing, in genuine friendship. It would have been more selfish not to share something of my own life, especially as he was asking me to do so.

During the last months of our correspondence I had been making a rather serious review of my own life, so I decided to tell Lesley about this. I had told very few people about any of it so it was good to confide in him and I could see that it meant a lot to him. I told him the story of my own personal vocation—how at the age of twenty-three, knowing that I had to give my life to God totally, I joined a missionary group of Sisters: the Missionary Sisters of Africa. After three years of training I had gone out to live in a remote part of Tanzania, Sumbawanga.

I had been extremely happy there, but had to return some years later as my parents were anxious to see me again. The Sisters wanted me to take a further degree. Leaving Tanzania was a terrible wrench; I loved every aspect of the country: the mountains, the vast empty spaces, but especially the people. I had spent my years working in a mission school where the children were boarders. There were seven of us in my community, and almost as many nationalities. I loved my young people. We were with them all day long and relationships were warm and full of fun. In the holidays we would go out to the various villages to visit their families.

Our aim as missionaries in Africa was always to prepare others to take our place: to make ourselves redundant. In my last years I worked closely with a great friend, a Tanzanian Sister who was to take over the middle school. We worked very happily together and it was hard to say goodbye.

The return to England was at first more of a culture shock than my first days in sun-filled Tanzania. I arrived in London on a bleak, grey, windy day. But at last I was back home in North Wales, and seeing the faces of my mother and father was just so wonderful.

I went to Lancaster University and obtained a degree in Theology. Several years in Liverpool followed, including seven as a chaplain at the university and two as a community worker in Toxteth. It was then that my mother, who already had cancer, was taken seriously ill. I knew I had no option but to return to Colwyn Bay to care for her. I did this with love until she died, five years later. By this time my father was in his nineties, so I could not leave him. I stayed on to be with him and care for him. It was at this juncture in my life that the correspondence with Lesley had begun. This much Lesley knew, and he had applauded me for it. He had cared for Wesley, his step grandfather, in his illness—right up to the time of the incident that cast him into death row.

During those years of caring for my parents my life had changed in subtle ways. Although it had been a radical change, leaving behind all the aspects of my life that I knew and loved, nevertheless I felt it to be a privilege to care for my parents who were two wonderful people. Gradually I built up a life in Wales again. When my father finally died, just before his hundredth birthday, I was faced with the second vocation challenge of my life. By now only a handful of British Sisters remained and most of those were in care homes or nursing homes. Somehow I could not find the impetus to impel me back to London to our community.

After three years of praying and reflecting, I felt that, if I were honest, I valued my base in North Wales too much to leave it. I contacted my local bishop to ask him if he would like to accept me as a Sister for his diocese. Bishop Edward Regan was enormously welcoming. And so, just before my second visit to Lesley, I had terminated my legal contract with the Sisters, to whom I remained affectionately attached, and became, instead of a Sister of Africa, a Sister of Wales!

This was the gist of what I shared with Lesley who listened with rapt attention, frequently nodding his head like a wise old father confessor. I asked him what he thought. With absolute wisdom he looked up and asked, "Are you happy?"

"Very!" I answered.

"Well!" he said, raising his hands as a big smile lit up his face. It was a lovely seal of approval.

As ever, the time sped by all too quickly and the visit was over. Before leaving we said goodbye by placing our hands on the glass, one over the other, either side. To my amazement, I heard Lesley saying, "I love you, Sister Joy."

I was very touched by this as in the past six or seven years Lesley had hardly used the word "love." I wondered if he had ever used it. It felt good. I responded with, "I love *you*, Lesley."

I walked from death row deep in thought. We had enjoyed our time together so much that for a while the reality of what was to happen had been blocked out.

Margôt was there to meet me. On the way home we noticed a little park and made a note of it, thinking how nice it would be to walk somewhere in the fresh air.

During our weeks in Texas we went from plane to car, from car to prison, from prison to malls or restaurants—and home again to air-conditioning. We who are used to the sea, the mountains and constant fresh air and exercise.

That evening I spoke at some length with Russell and Judith Perkins, Lesley's friends from New Hampshire. Russell had been corresponding with Lesley for about four years, and with his peaceful non-violent way of contemplation had a great impact on him. Judith, his wife, just a little older than us, was a lovely gentle person. They were followers of Sant Mat, but seemed to nourish their spiritual lives on Christian mystical writers, and Judith went off to their room to return with Russell's current collection of spiritual reading, all of it Christian. He was especially fond of Thomas Merton. I think we talked for almost two hours. We were deeply united through our friendship with Lesley, who had brought us together in correspondence some months before.

He was very pleased that we were all meeting together. If only he could have been with us.

9

Lesley Is Killed

It was 4:00 A.M. and I was wide awake. Sleep had been elusive. I lay on my bunk bed not wanting to disturb Margôt. By 5:00 A.M. we were both on the move. An immense feeling of powerlessness swept over me. Every fibre of my being was telling me that this person should not die. He should live to proclaim the miracle of the Lord's mercy, forgiveness and compassion. If only there were someone I could phone, someone who could stop this happening. Never in my entire life had I felt so totally, utterly helpless. The mother of Jesus must have felt like this as she became aware of the final chain of events leading to her son's execution. The Son of God himself could not prevent his own death. Like them, we were all caught up in a similar process and experiencing similar emotions.

As we get up, dress, drink coffee, clean our teeth . . . is Lesley doing the same? We will be alive this time tomorrow. Lesley will be dead. These thoughts are in our minds constantly, just as I imagine the thumping of a dreadful migraine must be. I can hardly remember, but I guess we helped ourselves to Bob's delicious warm rolls, always ready for us in the kitchen. There is a warm heart in Huntsville, and it is Hospitality House.

Now we are driving for the last time to Ellis One where I am allowed two final hours visiting Lesley. If only 6:00 P.M. on this day of 24 April 1998 would never come. The shadowy figures of the men in white and their horseback guards come into view. And now we are approaching the drive up to Ellis One. No matter how much we will it, time simply won't stop.

I say goodbye to Margôt for two hours, and for the last time go through all the routines. Even the staff seem subdued. Today is an execution day and they are only human. Lesley Gosch is liked and respected at Ellis One.

Ceidiog too has been going through his morning rituals. He was able to achieve a very successful interview with Lesley on Wednesday. He is an emotional person and it was a very big thing for him. Lesley had told me that Ceidiog was one of only two media people who came to death row with an open mind. He liked Ceidiog and Ceidiog liked him.

And so I find myself walking down to the very last booth, which this morning is mercifully quiet. In fact, everything seems unusually still. Kathryn Cox is already there, her Bible at the ready. But first there is some attempt at lighter talk. Somehow the conversation turns to flowers. Kathryn says to Lesley:

"Lesley, if Joy and I were flowers, what would we be?"

Lesley looks reflective. Before he's had time to answer, Kathryn bounces in: "I'm a Venus Fly-catcher! What's Joy?"

"Joy is a sunflower, definitely a sunflower!" says Lesley.

Then there is a silence. Lesley tells us there has been no word from the lawyers. He goes quiet. His head is propped up by his right hand. He is tired, so very tired. He knows the lawyers are working desperately and they too have not been sleeping. Hope is fading. He knows it. We know it. After a while, I see Kathryn opening her Bible and my stomach goes tight. She begins reading that wonderful passage from Romans 8:35–9.

> What shall separate us from the love of Christ? Can trouble do it, or hardship or persecution, or hunger or poverty or danger or death? No, in all these things we have complete victory through him who loved us! For I am certain that nothing can separate us from his love: neither death nor life; neither angels or other heavenly rulers or powers; neither the present nor the future; neither the world above nor the world below—there is nothing in all creation that will ever be able to separate us from the love of God which is ours through Christ Jesus our Lord.

Never had the power of words been so strong. Complete victory. For twelve years Lesley had suffered, prayed, struggled, cared for others, used so many of his talents to the full. His small body, with its several handicaps, housed a spirit that had come almost as far as any human being could come to "complete victory" and perfect love both for God and mankind. We looked upon a man about to enter the final stage of his passion. He was an utterly redeemed person who, in the last few years of his life and impending death, was surely a "co-redeemer" with Christ.

At this point my emotions, usually well controlled, went haywire. The tears flowed and wouldn't stop. This is awful, I thought to myself, the last thing that Lesley needs is to see me like this. It's too much. I am over-whelmed by the tragedy and at the same time by the beauty of the transformed life of the man in front of me.

So I got up and hid myself behind the Coke machine and just let go of my emotions. After a few seconds, I felt Kathryn's hand on my shoulder.

"Come back," she said gently, "it's good for Lesley to see you crying." I guess she was right. If someone cries for you, you really do know how much they care.

This is more than just caring. It is a sharing in the mystery of God's love, a deep entering into passion and compassion. I feel I am touching something way beyond my capacity to understand. All of this seems to be hap-pening inside me in a place that is beyond either thoughts or feelings. It is an experience of being right "inside" the mystery of love and redemption.

Some words from Kahlil Gibran's *The Prophet* float into my mind:

> Like the ocean is our God-self:
> It remains forever undefiled—
> Even like the sun is your God-self . . .

We sat silently for a while. Then Lesley leaned right over again, his head against his right hand. There is real sadness around now. I hear him saying: "I don't think I could go through it a fourth time." This is the third time he's had to face execution. How he has retained his wholeness and his sanity this far is a miracle. It's the first time he has spoken as though he truly believes it will happen. Up to now, hope had the upper hand, he really wanted to live. For a long time he had been promising to send me a painting he was doing of a Siberian snow tiger. Only yesterday he had said: "If I'm here on Saturday, I'm going to get down to finishing it." But somehow we all knew he wouldn't be here. I saw before me a man in the depths of human anguish, yet touched too by God's peace.

Time was ticking by.

Kathryn, as his regular spiritual adviser, was to have the privilege of spending a last half-hour with Lesley at The Walls, immediately prior to the execution, so she now excused herself and left me to have my last hour with him. He was extremely tired and was shifting from side to side on his steel stool. We at least had chairs to sit on. He explained to me how the prisoners had chairs at one time, but then one prisoner went berserk when his girlfriend was sent out for being too scantily dressed. The prisoner had smashed up his chair. The result was: no more chairs. Lesley still suffered considerable pain in his back and hips from the injuries that had been inflicted on him in his early childhood. It was hard for him sitting for long periods on the stool. A couple of times I had to fetch the guard to ask for him to be taken to the rest room. This means being led out of the cage in handcuffs. So very meekly. All of Lesley's struggles had been of a spiritual nature; he was not a very physical person at all.

We spoke about his birth mother. Yesterday I had asked him if he would like to see her. She lived near Houston and I was thinking that maybe we could go and fetch her. He looked at me and said, "Sister Joy [he nearly always called me *Sister* Joy], whatever I have wanted in my life I have never had." I somehow took this as a negative and was relieved. It might have been extremely tricky. Kathryn told me that his mother had been just once to visit him during his twelve years on death row and it had not gone too well. He told me her address. I told him we would try and find her. He said everyone would know her. When I told Margôt, she agreed that we should look her up on the way to the airport.

And so the minutes ticked relentlessly on. Lesley was very quiet and subdued. They brought him a meal and he picked at it. There was even a cake. He touched it with his fork and explained that he wouldn't be eating it as it contained egg. To the very end, he remained a strict vegetarian. At 10:30 Greg, the friend from Houston, was coming for half-an-hour. I dreaded saying the final goodbye. We were very quiet now . . . all too aware of what was soon to happen. How can there be any right words to utter as life is about to be cut short? When Jesus' friends in Gethsemane fell asleep, were they simply escaping from what was unendurable? I told him I would be with him every step of the way on his last journey. Words can sound so banal. I had never felt so terrible in my whole life. Why couldn't we save him? Surely they couldn't really want to kill Lesley.

I see Greg approaching. So this is it. I stay for a couple of minutes with Greg, then I stand. The usual hand on glass. And he said it again,

"I love you, Sister Joy."

"I love you, Lesley."

His love for me was the simple, almost childlike gratitude to one who cared about him unconditionally and was ready to travel around twenty thousand miles simply to be with him. The love I had for him was based on admiration of his courage and wisdom; and so much else besides. A most extraordinary friendship.

It was no good hoping for a last glance from Lesley. He wouldn't have been able to see me even if he had tried.

I walked through the visiting hall, the reception, the gates and out into the sunshine. For Lesley, there would be a hot fifteen-mile ride in a van to The Walls prison.

Thank God for Margôt who was there waiting for me; we drove off. Farewell Ellis One. Margôt was very hot from waiting in the parking lot; I was freezing. Without Margôt this experience would have been unbearable.

It was like Good Friday. We had some light refreshment in Huntsville, then drove back to Hospitality House—a short rest, a cup of coffee here, a few words there. Bernie and her mother gave us looks of great empathy. Mrs. Cannon was still drowsy with Valium-induced sleep.

Then at 5:00 P.M. down to The Walls prison. The six of us—Kathryn, myself, the couple from Houston, Russell and Judith—were escorted to the prison by the establishment chaplains who remained with us throughout. Neither Lesley nor Ted had ever spoken of them; their presence was a prison routine. We were taken into The Walls prison. It was so surreal. During the several vigils at which I had been present I had seen the victims' families being taken to the Death House. Now I was one of them. Margôt was outside holding banners with the other protesters.

Our guards were extremely courteous, opening all the doors and telling us to "mind the step." One of them, I couldn't help noticing, had rather a kind face. He almost looked ashamed. I have since prayed for him a few times as he looked so out of place. The others I have no recollection of.

We were led through several corridors and electronic doors. First we were taken to a small room to be searched. This was done by a pleasant young woman, who kept laughing nervously because the instrument with which she frisked us wasn't working properly.

Next we found ourselves in a waiting area. We sat round a table and a man in a dark suit went through the briefing session yet again. I switched off, longing for him to stop. Lesley, we knew, would by now be deep in meditation and we just wanted to be in union with him. My thoughts momentarily flashed to North Wales where some of our friends, Anne, Peter, Liz and Millie, had organized a vigil for Lesley in our parish. They had put a lot of thought into their choice of prayers, music and readings.

The man in the suit sat at a table writing copious notes. Whatever could he be writing? From then on I looked at no one, I closed into myself and to God, to that inner sanctuary no other can enter, but where all can be found. Lesley knew we would be deeply in prayer in union with him. There we all sat with our heads bent over, in absolute stillness. It must have been a bit unusual as the local paper later commented on it. We stayed like that for about thirty-five minutes. It was a very powerful experience, very strengthening for all of us, and I believe it was the same for Lesley. There had been so many efforts to save Lesley. Now it was the moment when all activity had ceased and we just had to be with him as he made his final journey into the eternal joys of heaven.

Suddenly a man was beckoning us to move forward. As though on autopilot, we stood and moved as one, looking at no one, still in total silence. Like speechless people in the land of the dead. There was Lesley in pure white on a mattress of white, strapped down from head to foot. Even his wrists were bound with white bandages, a procedure I had been told was absolutely unnecessary and not always carried out. It was hard to believe that the killing had started. I looked at Lesley's stomach going up and down, the breathing appearing so normal. Then it was as though he were giving a little suppressed cough. But it was no cough, his lungs were being shattered. All of us gazed in continued hushed stillness. Suddenly a medic appeared and started checking him over with a stethoscope. We heard a voice pronouncing: "Death occurred at 6:38 P.M." So that is it. Lesley Gosch, loved by many, is dead. It is so final, death. They have had their way. He had said he felt no bitterness. In my weekly hospital visits in North Wales I regularly walk past white-coated doctors with stethoscopes hanging around their necks. Doctors dedicated to saving lives. I cannot see them now without remembering that doctor of death.

We were led out, again with absolute courtesy. I know that Judith, Russell, Kathryn and I were weeping inwardly, but we were totally in control so as to show no sign of weakness to the members of the Texas Criminal "Justice" system. Finally we arrived at the last electronically controlled door; we would soon be outside with the sun on our faces again. Lesley was now away from this awful place of injustice and retribution. Now his vision would be restored, his transformed body whole, his pains gone. Long live Lesley (to quote my godson Michael Wright). Michael had taken Lesley to heart and had written him several letters, as had his younger brother Joseph.

We were asked by the guards if we would like to be escorted to any place. Did they think that, as Lesley's friends, we would be attacked or something? We politely declined their offer and found our way over to the vigil site. We, his six witnesses, hugged Judith and Russell who were leaving for New Hampshire, and Greg and his wife who were returning to Houston. We were beyond words. When they had driven off, Kathryn Cox asked me if I would go with her to the funeral parlor as she anticipated some difficulty. It was she who organized everything concerning Lesley's remains, which were to be kept refrigerated until Monday when he would be cremated. His ashes would be sent to the care of his Uncle Lloyd Heron, about whom I had heard quite a lot from Lesley. It took us quite some time to find the place.

When we did find it, the male prison chaplain was on the doorstep. As we entered he offered us a sweet. I still have that unwrapped sweet marked Funeral Parlor. A sweet for a life.

He said, "How y'all doin'?"

I replied, "I'm puzzled."

A few moments later he pursued this with, "What's puzzling you?"

I had such deep anger within and I heard myself replying, "You kill people so nicely here."

The poor man looked as though an electric bolt had hit him. The last time I saw him he seemed very deep in thought.

We were now inside the funeral parlor.

"Look Joy, Lesley is here!"

Kathryn calls me over to a spacious area where Lesley is lying, just as we had seen him in the death room. I had not expected this; it was a complete surprise.

"Lesley, are you playing a trick on us? Are you still here?" No response. We both kissed him on the forehead and left.

The business of refrigeration concluded, we returned to Hospitality House. On the way there Kathryn gave me the unfinished painting of the Siberian snow tiger that she had kept safely for me. Back at Hospitality House, Ceidiog and Marcus were waiting for the last interviews for Welsh TV. We went down the road to do the work near a little, almost hidden, shrine to the Indians who had been wiped off the map by the new Texans. Kathryn Cox was also interviewed for the film. She says she can never agree with death row. "Eye for eye, tooth for tooth," she reminds everyone, "makes the whole world blind and toothless." She adds, "No one deserves to die like that, especially Lesley. When they killed him, they killed a part of me."

This interview concluded, it was time to say goodbye to Ceidiog and Marcus, who would now return to Houston. Marcus, a true Texan, had been genuinely moved over the past few days and asked Ceidiog for a copy of the entire tape. I have always hoped he found a way to show it in Texas. After all, people over there need to see it far more than the people of Wales. Marcus asked us to visit his home and family in Houston if we should one day find the time. He said he had friends in Wales, so there was the usual "hope to see you again." By this stage Ceidiog was exhausted, and was due to fly back to London on the following Sunday after sorting out his tapes. There were some very warm hugs, and then they were all gone.

It was very much like a good Friday evening. Everyone seemed to be gone, including Kathryn, now on the 180-mile drive home to Dallas. We all felt concerned for her.

But Hospitality House was still there. I lay in my bunk that night thinking only of Lesley. Margôt was doing the same.

A couple of months later, Garry wrote to me:

I'm glad to know that you were able to see and touch Lesley at the funeral home. I heard, from some of the guys who visit with Kathy Cox, that when she had gone to pick up his ashes she had stopped here on the way back to visit one of her regulars, and she had his ashes outside. I bet Lesley would have gotten a good laugh with that. He got to come, and leave, without anyone trying to handcuff him (smile).

10

The Last Mission in Texas

And so a new day dawned, a day heavy with the overwhelming sorrow of what had been done the previous day. We breakfasted with three cheerful black children and their beautiful mother, who looked absolutely gorgeous in readiness for visiting her husband. The children seemed blissfully unaware of exactly where they were going. They were just excited to be seeing their father.

Also at breakfast were a dear old couple in their eighties, from near Dallas. The lady could not walk very well so her husband pottered about the kitchen seeing to her every need. Their son had a thirty-year sentence, so they would spend their lives until they died like this, knowing he would never walk through their door again.

Back in our room Margôt and I began sorting our things and preparing for our departure. While I had been with Lesley the previous day, Margôt had been making some good contacts and gathering telephone numbers and addresses of people to network with. These were precious and had to be kept safely.

Before leaving Huntsville I had something important to do. This was to phone Lesley's Uncle Lloyd, the brother of his granny who had adopted him. Lloyd was the one and only family member who had kept in contact with Lesley. With his wife Mary, he lives in Colorado and is a retired university professor. Lesley had written to me about him and I had formed a picture of a very good man. Before Lesley's execution I had promised him I would call Uncle Lloyd.

On that sad Saturday morning, 25 April, I called him. He was delighted, and sounded every bit as pleasant as I had imagined him. I was able to tell him how graciously and peacefully Lesley accepted his death and how he was totally forgiving of his killers. Uncle Lloyd listened intently. "It should never have been this way," he said. "If he had had a good lawyer at his trial, he would never have gone to death row." I wished we could have met face to face and had a long talk about the details of Lesley's past. I told him how our HTV newsman had come over from Wales and recorded a fifteen-minute interview with Lesley and that, all being well, I would send him a copy of this tape. He was very pleased about that.

I was in fact able to do this so that he, like us, now has Lesley "live" on tape for ever. Lesley had been overjoyed at seeing Uncle Lloyd in January. Lloyd was to have been with him during the execution on that date . . . a date that left Lesley alive. The visit had been very special as Lloyd had been able to fill Lesley in regarding his early childhood, an area that was full of confusion in his memory and about which he never spoke—until after that visit from Lloyd. It was wonderful for me to speak to Lloyd; he was a live link with Lesley.

There was no longer anything to keep us in Huntsville and we longed to be away from the place. Our plane left on Monday, but we decided to leave Huntsville on the Sunday morning and take our time, looking up Lesley's mother on the way to Houston. We would stay overnight in Houston and have a rest before returning home.

On Sunday mornings, Hospitality House is closed till 1:00 P.M. as the staff and others spend all morning at church. So we went for a brunch and left Huntsville behind us.

We found our way without difficulty to the small town where we hoped to find Lesley's birth mother, Rose. There were five thousand-plus houses in the street we were looking for. It was 1:00 P.M. Everywhere was quiet and not a soul was in sight. After driving for a while we spotted a man in a garage. We stopped and asked if by any chance he knew where Rose lived.

"She's right here!" And out walked the mother who gave Lesley away at two years of age when she was just eighteen years old. A smallish lady, fifty-eight now, with short grey hair.

I immediately explained who we were: that I was a Catholic nun and a great friend of Lesley, and that this was my friend Margôt. She was looking a little bit startled and nervous, and later explained that she thought we might be inspectors. Ironically, she runs a day-care center for a dozen toddlers, and inspectors drop in at any time. She said, "Lesley's on death row, isn't he?"

Margôt and I looked at each other, both realizing that she had no idea that he'd been killed two days previously. (I later learned from Lesley's Uncle Lloyd that he had informed her about the 15 January execution date, but she had said that she was so busy she wouldn't be able to go.) Gradually, we found a way of telling her the facts. A small tear appeared and then she began to show us her house, her family photos, everything. She appeared to be blocking it all out. We gazed at the beautiful faces lining the walls.

"Do you have any pictures of Lesley?"

"Lesley? No, I don't think I do."

She then showed us all the tax return forms she had been in the middle of working on, the many jars of children's food and drink that lined the shelves of her cupboards; the rooms, and the toys of the children. Sam, her husband, had Parkinson's disease. A daughter, son-in-law and two little grand-daughters lived with them. Down the road was her eighty-five-year-old mother whom she also tried to look after, but for whom she could not do as much as she would have liked. The son-in-law didn't work, slept half the day, and ate her out of house and home. This was a very harassed lady. Having scant financial resources and few places to turn for help, her fears and worries were real. Her life had never produced much happiness, a cycle that was repeated in Lesley's story.

After about half-an-hour we all sat down in the kitchen: Rose, Margôt and myself. The daughter did not seem interested and we had the feeling that she thought we were state officials. We had a cold drink, and at last Rose asked about the son she had given birth to forty-two years ago at the age of sixteen.

We were able to tell her very good and positive things about him. Her tears started flowing. "And I never found time to go to him." In a letter the previous year, Lesley had told me how he had forgiven his mother. "I know from experience how hard life can be," he had said.

I was able to tell Rose about this. She then told us how she had had a breakdown, had become an alcoholic and a heavy smoker, but that now she had come through it all.

All her life she had borne the guilt of having given her son away. Margôt and I both felt it had been right for us to go to see her, and that we were used as instruments of healing. Lesley was now at peace and Rose could be too.

Sam came in and took a photo of the three of us together. As we left, both Sam and Rose had big smiles on their faces. Rose asked me to write to her and I have since done so.

11

Home Again

Having spent time with Lesley's birth mother, our mission in Texas was all but complete. After a good night's rest at Day's Inn, the last hurdle was finding our way through Houston's maze of freeways to return our car to the rental company. Not pleasant! One mistake can send you hurtling all around the city again—and not just once! At the car rental company we had our last death-penalty conversation. It was with the young man with whom we were dealing. As usual, he was fairly strong in his "pro" views.

But after talking for a few minutes he was already mellowing, and told us that in Britain we are more "civilized." The openness of the average American is impressive. Sr. Helen Prejean, author of *Dead Man Walking*, recently said that American support for the death penalty is "a million miles wide but only an inch deep." I truly believe that. Perhaps Americans are suffering from a collective paranoia brought on by daily flooding of crime news by the media. "They love their fear," said one shop assistant. "Take away their fear and they wouldn't know what to do."

On our last trip by road to the airport we were with a party of British water-skiers returning from what had obviously been a wonderful vacation in Texas. When they heard what we had been doing, they were astounded. One woman in particular seemed quite moved.

Once inside the airport lounge we had about an hour to wait. As we wandered toward the shops, who should come walking toward us but two of the Italians we had met at Hospitality House who had been there for Jo Cannon's execution. They told us how pleased they were to see us because they had wanted to tell us that they had tried to get over to Huntsville from Houston for Lesley's execution on the Friday. However, the traffic had been so bad, due to an accident, that they couldn't make it in time, and consequently they had felt really bad about it. We marveled at this chance meeting at the airport. Again it was an experience of the warmth and love felt by all who share in this unusual mission or ministry. There is so much sadness, but so much enrichment too. More big hugs.

At last we are on the plane. We take off. It's reflection time. No words could ever adequately describe the many thoughts and feelings of a week like this one. On the Wednesday they killed a brain-damaged man who, after nineteen years on death row, had found the stability and routine in his life that had been denied him in the free world. He was totally institutionalized and harmless. I have never before witnessed grief quite like that of his mother and sister.

Lesley was dead. On the Friday they killed a brilliant and deeply spiritual man with several physical handicaps: Lesley was registered blind, was partially deaf, had lost most of his fingertips, and suffered constant back pain as a result of abuse in early childhood. On death row he became a man of wisdom, respected by all, including some of the guards.

Lesley had introduced me to a world I had heard about, but would never have dreamed of becoming so deeply involved in. He showed me what must be the full extent of a person's ability to triumph over every conceivable setback, pain, insult, hardship, deprivation and injustice. Even though widely believed to be innocent of murder, Lesley, like the rest of humankind, was no saint the day he was led to death row. He became a saint, or at least a saintly person, during his time there.

His anger and bitterness were, with God's help and his own response, turned into love and acceptance. He had his moments of darkness and despair, and in a sense it can be said that darkness was the backdrop to his life on death row. But it was a darkness illuminated by the great light of God's love which transformed his days and nights and made him such an inspiration to all.

Friends who came to know Lesley after his incarceration in Huntsville all bear witness to his fine moral character. Kathryn Cox stated without hesitation that Lesley was "an intelligent, philosophical and deeply spiritual individual." This too was my experience of knowing Lesley. Never will I forget our conversations in which he showed himself to be widely read and reflective. His artwork is remarkable. He was, I felt, a person who on death row had found himself and his God, and as a result was at peace with himself.

How could his execution have happened? Was it really true or was it all a bad dream from which we would awake? As we flew nearer to Europe, we both felt comforted. We felt we were coming home to a kinder, more compassionate world.

The images of the week float freely through my mind. Throughout them all is Margôt, my wonderful friend and confidante. A newspaper would later describe us as "sisters of mercy on a humanitarian mission." We really have become like sisters as well as friends. We go back a long way, having been for a while at the same school and later at the same college. Our parents knew each other. Her father had been a great comfort to mine as he approached the end of his life. After my father's death, I loved to visit Carl (short for Caradoc), her father. Margôt and I had been there for each other in the loss of both sets of parents. That's the sort of friendship that is indestructible. And now we are in this death row life together. I have lost my first prisoner-friend and she too could lose hers—but we try not to think about that.

This second week in Texas would have been very difficult to bear alone. Together we were powerfully aware of God's constant love and strength through every minute of it. Our shared faith and trust in a loving God is what transforms every aspect of this grim scenario. Lesley's spirit of forgiveness, his calm strength, even in weakness; the light in Ted's eyes, the unbelievable frankness with which Garry told me of his crime; the humor and practical love and care of Kathryn Cox toward all her prisoners, and toward Lesley in particular, the patient love and devotion of all death row families; the quiet sorrow and strong faith of Maggie whose son was killed the previous Easter after twenty-three years on death row. These images float free.

I reflected too on the families of the murder victims. Ceidiog had managed to interview Mr. Patton and his daughter at some length, though I had not had the opportunity of meeting either of them. I was, at that moment, on my way to the funeral parlor with Kathryn Cox.

Once back home, I have been able to watch them many times on video tape. Mr. Patton comes across as a kind and gentle man. He had once expressed the desire to meet Lesley. He spoke about his wife's killing as having been a terrible capital murder and how society has to have laws and punishments commensurate with the crimes. He looked more sad than vengeful.

His daughter said that Lesley's killing was not revenge, it was justice. She said how, as a biologist, she was mainly concerned with the effects of the three lethal chemicals on Lesley's body. Believing the original conviction, she had waited twelve years for the twenty or so minutes on 24 April 1998 when she could stand and witness her mother's alleged killer receive his ultimate punishment. For twelve years she must have suffered the most unbearable pain, and who could blame her for wanting Lesley dead.

Indeed, if the road back to wholeness is a long and arduous one for the death row prisoners, what of the long road back to healing that must be traveled by the victims' families?

One thing is certain: witnessing another death is not helpful to the healing process. What is helpful? It is important that the victims' families know that the perpetrators of crime do receive real and possibly long-term punishment. It is equally important that the state and others provide all possible help, support and counseling, for as long as is needed, to victims' families.

Ultimately, I reflected, it is only an awareness of God's love that can heal both the victim's family and the criminal himself. This love is normally mediated through other loving, caring, compassionate human beings.

I remember the young Italian men and women at Hospitality House, their warmth, love and intelligent concern. Back in Italy, they too are working to end the death penalty. So many images. Last, but not least, Pastor Bob at Hospitality House—his quiet, smiling, unobtrusive presence and welcoming personality make him the ideal person to run a house whose slogan is "Help for Hurting Families." His wife Nelda is a rock of support to him and is also a very practical person. His pastoral assistant, Jean, is perfect for the job: smiling, discreet, available.

The memories of the execution vigils can never be forgotten. It had been especially moving to speak with families of murder victims who were against the death penalty. We were so inspired by them. Neither of us will ever forget speaking with the brother of one of Karla Faye Tucker's victims; he had turned his life around from one of anger and bitterness to become a person filled with forgiveness. He told me, "I cry for my sister every day, but I don't want any more people to die. I am totally opposed to execution as a means of punishment. I am a Christian so I cannot believe in things like that, but most of all because I am a human being."

On the evening of Lesley's execution, Sue Lusk called us from Florida. Sue is the Texas co-ordinator for Human Writes and she has become a great friend. She followed us to Hospitality House a few days later to visit her friend Cliff Boggess, a wonderful Christian, executed on 11 June 1998 on his thirty-third birthday. I remember Sam and Danny, the two warm-hearted student waiters at the Golden Corral who were so helpful to us. I remember all the people we met at the vigils, especially Betty Mathews. And how Margôt worked so hard at making contacts. I remember how the guards respected Lesley, and his respect for them as fellow human beings. Death row itself I can never forget. The figures in white as they approach their visiting booths looking for all the world like contemplative monks. And their loved ones, trying to put on a brave face in the midst of such anguish. I can't help remembering the scene at the funeral parlor and how the official chaplain offered me a sweet. A sweet for a life. And then how Kathryn and I saw and touched Lesley's warm body. Above all, it is Lesley Gosch who tends to fill the spaces of my mind. Lesley who was so alive, so profound.

It was Lesley who opened up this new undreamed-of world to us when he wrote that card in the August of 1997: "The one thing I would ask of you is that you would come on a visit and witness to the world about what is happening here." So we went—Margôt and I. And now we are both totally committed to witnessing to the world. How? As we spoke about it on the plane, we just knew that each new step would be shown to us, just as had happened so far. Love would direct our steps.

Another half-hour and we would be arriving at Gatwick.

Now we are at Manchester.

Now at home in North Wales.

Margôt and I have said goodbye, and I am greeted by Sister Mary who has been making her retreat and praying for us every day. We hug one another. Now I'm hugging my cat. After a chat, a meal and watching the news, my eyelids are closing and soon I'm in a deep, deep sleep. In the morning, the moment I awake the vision of Lesley on the gurney is there in front of me. It will take a long time before the images fade, if ever.

That morning the phone rings and of course it is Margôt. It's as if we need to talk to each other frequently as we are the only ones around who fully understand. I had read *Dead Man Walking* and seen the film before going to Texas. There is nothing to compare with actually being there. The experience is unique and extraordinary; I keep coming back to the word "surreal." But also, it was all very real. I keep asking myself how American politicians have the stomach for this cold calculated killing . . . how can medics and others keep killing people . . . how can they sleep at night? Do they go home and tell their wives and children, "Today I killed again"? These murders are far, far worse than those committed in the heat of the moment by those on death row. *Poor.* Black. Hispanic. Men and women who have usually suffered abuse and dysfunctional families, men and women who are nobodies.

12

Post Texas

It was good to fall into the rhythm of normal life again, catching up with local activities. But Texas was never far from the surface of our minds and always in the deeper places of our hearts.

The very next week Margôt and I were invited to speak to a hundred sixth graders in Birmingham. The staff and pupils at that Catholic secondary school were very welcoming and interested in all we had to share with them.

Soon we were being invited to speak in several other secondary schools in North Wales and to various groups: nurses working with terminally ill patients, college groups, religious communities and others. We were now used to hearing the same comments, "It's barbaric!" and questions such as, "Why do they keep them so long before they kill them?" People nearly always wanted to know what crimes our friends had committed or if the person was innocent. If we say Lesley was innocent, they want to know how we know he was innocent. In fact, we never tell anyone anything about a person's crime as this is very confidential information. Thankfully, the vast majority of people here in Wales seem to share our anti-death-penalty views, though I guess those who think otherwise wouldn't tell us. But we have had enormous support and continue to have it.

Two weeks after Lesley was executed, the flute he had made for me finally arrived. I wish it had arrived while he was still alive, so that I could have thanked him for it properly. It is a very beautifully crafted flute based on the type used by the American Indians. It will of course always remain one of my most cherished possessions.

In May, I received this reflection from Garry:

```
You said you were interested in how I
remember Lesley. He was a fairly private
person. He was almost always friendly,
rarely showed any temper or aggravation he
was experiencing. That in itself is amazing.
Everyone here goes through bouts of frustra-
tion or anger on a frequent basis. It's the
price you pay for living in such close quar-
ters with people who are at odds with your
own personality. Lesley was able to contain
his well, you rarely knew when or if he was
angry. He was also very generous and giving
of both his time and whatever he had. The
main thing I liked about Lesley, though, was
his sense of humor.
```

The newspapers followed up our story, especially the *Daily Post*. We have a lot to thank the journalist Ian Lang for, and his mentor Mr. Iorweth Roberts.

The radio stations asked us for interviews, and Granada TV made a half-hour film.

Meanwhile, Ceidiog Hughes of HTV had kindly given us a copy of his tape so that we have Lesley recorded for posterity. It was a good interview. On the tape we see Ceidiog asking Lesley if he feels angry and bitter about what they were about to do to him. He reflects for a moment and gives his answer: "When I first came to death row, yes, I felt anger. But now, because of things that have happened in my life since I came here—no—I don't feel anger toward those people. I don't hate them . . . but I feel sorry for them. You have to respect them because they are other human beings. They are only doing their job." He went on, "I hope that everybody who thinks they are going to feel better if I am killed . . . I hope they do. But I think they are going to find it doesn't solve anything."

Lesley goes on to say that there are too many people making capital out of capital punishment. Statistics show that capital punishment is not an effective deterrent, and that it costs a lot more to execute a person (because of the expense of the appeals procedure) than it does to keep them in prison for life.

Ceidiog asks him how he copes with the emotions of knowing that in all probability he is about to be killed. Lesley explains that it is not so much terror of what might happen, he just wanted to get it over with so that he could get on with his life—either here on earth, once all the uncertainty had ended, or in life after death, if he was killed. He says how on death row you get into a routine and suddenly when your date comes up your whole life goes into a "giant jumble" and everything turns to chaos: "It's not so much that you're afraid of dying; after all, it's one of the few things in life you can't mess up [smile].

There *is* fear, you can't help it. I'd say anybody who goes over to The Walls and says they weren't scared is either crazy or a liar. I've been over there twice and I was scared both times. You can sit in your cell and say, 'I'm going to do this and I'm going to do that,' but when you get over there it's all different."

Ceidiog asked him how he coped with such a roller-coaster of emotions. Lesley answered, "You get over there and you're wired up, so tense. You don't notice that every muscle in your body is just as tight as it will go and your stomach has to untwist a couple of times to get tighter. And after you get back to your cell and finally relax, you feel like someone beat you all over with a baseball bat."

Asked by Ceidiog if he would like another stay of execution he said, "Sure I'd like a stay. I think everybody wants to keep on living. I'm ready for whatever comes. It's going over there with hope that makes that journey *so* difficult. If you go over there with the idea 'I'm going to die today,' it's much easier. What causes all the difficulty is not knowing."

The final question was, "What would you like to say to the people of Wales?"

"I'd like to thank all those who put in a good word for me. Sister Joy and Margôt are battling not only for me, but for all the people on death row. Ingrained as the death penalty is in the minds of people over here, it's going to take a lot of people to get it stopped. Whatever you do, don't ever bring the death penalty back to your country. You'll only be doing something you'll be sorry for later."

The interview was one that Ceidiog will never forget.

The most important activity of all for Margôt and myself remains the writing of letters to our friends on death row. My new correspondence with Garry has got off the ground, and Margôt will soon be celebrating the two-year anniversary of her friendship with Ted. Lesley will always be special for me, but I am now enjoying getting to know Garry. His story must wait to be told later. He is expecting his first execution date in the near future.

Ted also writes to me from time to time. In August 1998 he wrote:

I do hope you're not dwelling too much on Lesley's execution and the tragedy of his life. He would want you to be happy. He's a winner, a champion who faced challenges most people will never imagine—and he beat them. He wasn't much to look at, at least by society's standards, and his entire life may seem a total waste, but he died with a good heart and his soul is beautiful. The man they executed was not the same man they sentenced to die. If he had been sentenced to ten years of love and compassion and mercy, I think he would have made a great impression on the world, or at least a small part of it.

Lesley's story is not rare though. You might be surprised at the great number of truly good people on death row. But they never had the opportunity to let that goodness out, and now they probably never will.

In your work with children and young people you have a chance, perhaps, to stop someone becoming a Lesley, a Cliff or a me. Push them, encourage them, dare to tell them, "No!" God knows, I wish I could.

I would say that you were very privileged to have Lesley say, "I love you, Sister Joy."

```
I can't recall that he ever claimed to love
anyone. He believed that we should love God
who dwells in each person, but to actually
love the person is to make yourself vulner-
able. You must have touched his heart in a
very special way. I'm glad you were his
friend.
```

Our own story continues. We remain committed to carrying out any activity that can help in even the smallest way to contributing to the end of the death penalty, which causes so much distress to so many. Whenever invited, Margôt and I willingly speak about our experiences and our views; we feel sure that God is with us because we seem to be successful in this. People are moved. Many want to help. Sometimes people want to join Human Writes. We always suggest that they give themselves plenty of time to think about it as it is a big commitment, not best made on the spur of the moment.

My final reflection is this: through all of the events around and between our two visits to Texas, we both feel that we have been caught up in an extraordinary experience of redemption. We have learned just how important it is not to take things at face value. Many people in Texas told us about the monsters of death row: "There are real bad people in there." In reality, there are no monsters. There are terribly hurt, wounded people who, at some unfortunate moment in their lives, have lashed out at another human being and killed them. This is terrible. To kill is terrible. But most murders are not cold and calculated like those perpetrated by the state of Texas.

A great number of men and women on death row sincerely and genuinely change and become good people because they have consciously looked inward. Seeing the more violent aspects of their nature they have struggled to grow and to change. Many succeed, our friends among their number. They become redeemed people, and I firmly believe that through their courage and efforts they deeply affect those of us who visit them. It is an all-round redemption. The glory of death row is also an ongoing, living monument to forgiveness. Having repented, our friends learn to live in the sunshine of God's forgiveness. They in turn learn to forgive their tormentors. It's a long slow path but it happens, and it is truly wonderful. So we too, their friends and visitors, are caught up in a cycle of redemption and forgiveness, whose source is in the compassionate heart of God.

It also has to be remembered that some men and women on death row are entirely innocent of the crime for which they have been convicted.

After visiting death row, so many things in life seem banal. Our friends have touched the extreme limits of evil and goodness and we have been there with them.

Those trips to Texas have been costly in terms of energy and anguish, but neither Margôt nor myself would have missed them for anything. Our initial "yes" to Lesley's invitation was the start of a new chapter in our lives in which many unexpected friendships flourished and will continue to do so. We had traveled a strange and unusual road. We had stumbled into a world so far removed from our own.

Thank you, Lesley, for opening up this world to all of us—a place of hell, but where heaven constantly breaks through. Before leaving for Texas, a Jesuit friend had said, "Let love direct your steps." Prophetic words. Love directed, is directing and will direct.

Epilogue

If this story has seemed a sad one, it is because what is happening in Texas and elsewhere in the U. S. is sad in the extreme. In spite of that, our friends on death row can laugh (Garry loves cartoons) and they give so much to us. They are more spiritually alive than almost anyone I know out in the free world. They have to keep hoping. First they hope to be spared a death sentence. When they receive it, they try to fix their eyes on heaven.

We too have to keep the fires of hope burning.

Slavery was eventually abolished. The barbaric practice of the death penalty will also end one day. The Americans, after all, are not barbarians, so surely they will come to listen to what the rest of the world is saying to them. We have to believe this. There are so many groups and organizations in both the U.S.A. and beyond working toward this end. The end of the death penalty cannot come soon enough, but it *will* come.

Margôt and I have now been on a third visit to Texas to visit Ted, Garry and a new twenty-five-year-old, Anthony. In December 1998 there was a foiled escape attempt in which one prisoner was shot and later died of his injuries. Other prisoners knew nothing of this incident, but severe punishments were meted out, leaving our friends dejected and frustrated, even though an official inquiry found that the break-out was ninety percent due to security failure.

It has now been decided to move the entire death row unit of 450 men to a new "supermax" prison forty-five miles away, where there will be no human contact.

On our third visit we were enormously encouraged to find that everywhere we went attitudes had changed dramatically. We hardly found anyone anywhere in Texas who still wanted the death penalty. They told us, "We are sick of it. There has to be another way." We couldn't believe it, it was such a turnaround.

Meanwhile, Lesley's ashes have been scattered in the Laguna Madre Bay where he used to fish as a boy. It was a simple service presided over by Kathryn Cox, Uncle Lloyd and his family.

Lesley is finally at peace.

No Hope?

Staring at the wall, memories turn into fantasy
of a world that could have been, but never will
  be.
Memories burned into my mind of shattered
  dreams.
Worlds passing me by, no hope it seems.

Mail call's just gone by; what's the use.
Too many broken hearts. I have no excuse.
Weekend's over. No visits again.
If only I could see what could have been.

Never had anybody to love me. Nobody to
  care.
No love to give, only hate to share.
No hope, no hope, the walls echo over again.
Reduced to an animal, no longer a man.

The hours seem like days, the days like years.
The torment's unbearable, all that's left is tears.

I turn to the wall for a last refrain
with the repeated echo "NO HOPE" once again.

I had a Bible that I'd never read
nothing else to do. "What's to lose?" I said.
I'm tired of games, this time's for real.
As I started to read I began to feel
the words come to life. Never heard *this* before.
Yes, there IS hope, and so much more.
Someone to love me, someone to care.
Now when I need Him He's always there.

The walls no longer contain my soul
as I soar to dreams of a bigger goal.
No longer the torment, no longer the fear
now the walls echo the words "Hope is here."

As I walk down the hall a man passes by
the words "no hope," a tear in his eye.
Hope of the hopeless, Jesus my friend
He is the answer—those fears can end.

Now I have another with whom I can share
and we have more friends, someone to care
Loneliness is gone, there *is* hope you see!
The mail call is here. A letter for me!

                    Eddie Grisson, Texas death row

  This poem reflects the change from despair to
joy—brought about by the discovery of God's love and
the gift of a friend.

Acknowledgments

First thanks absolutely have to go to John Perrett.

John, you gave so very many hours of your time as we sat together at your computer. Your efficiency and generosity were endless. I'm sure both of us will always remember that one special moment when we had a strong feeling of Lesley's presence hovering just behind us. God bless you, John, as you embark on your career.

Very many thanks to Joan Head and her family for all the typing. This helped so much to get things started. You gave of your time, Joan, with much cheerfulness and generosity.

Thanks to Margôt for accompanying me, and for so much more besides, and not forgetting John, her husband, who always showed great interest. Many, many thanks to Sue Lusk, our wonderful Human Writes Texas co-ordinator. Sue, you are an unfailing source of support and inspiration to all of us. Many thanks also to Nick Ashton for setting up the Website, and for the e-mail address.

Thank you, Sr. Mary Dumbrill, for looking after Beauty during our second visit to Texas.

Jan Arriens, thank you for Human Writes, without which we would never have come to know our special friends at Ellis One.

Many thanks to you, dear Lynn Caddick, for your careful reading, and thanks too to Anna Perry, Mary and Paul Pinkman, Anne and Peter Hardisty, Millie, Mary Moxam, Elizabeth Harris, Dr. Martina Barrett-Nnochiri and Dr. Caroline Freeman, and to Ruth Eidenberg, for your enthusiasm and encouragement.

Special thanks to Norma and Mike Wright, who whole-heartedly supported Lesley and are now involved with others at Ellis One. Thanks too to Michael and Joseph.

Many thanks to Lesley's lawyers, Raoul Schonemann and Maurie Levin, for their many, many faxes and e-mails during the difficult days; also for sharing documents and for working so hard on Lesley's behalf.

Many thanks to the Sisters of Africa, the community at Saint Beuno's (especially Michael Ivens), and the Carmelite Sisters in Liverpool.

Thanks, Gerry J., you were always there.

Thank you, Fr. McGhee, parish priest of Saint Joseph's, for your music at the vigil and for your interest.

All our friends in the media were wonderful. They became almost personally involved in Lesley's predicament. Thank you, Ian Lang, for getting the ball rolling. Ceidiog, you were quick to take up the story. Thank you so much for coming all that way to Texas and capturing Lesley on film.

And a big thank you to all who wrote letters to try and save Lesley.

A Note about Human Writes

At the present time, more than 3,700 people are condemned to death in the U.S.A., most facing many years on death row prior to execution.

Human Writes is an English non-profit organization, which was founded with the purpose of offering non-judgmental friendship through letter writing to people on death row, some of whom no longer have contact with their families or friends and little or no links with the outside world. Receiving letters can make a real difference to their lives and many of them speak of their penfriends as their "windows to the world." Equally, penfriends usually find that the frienships they develop are very rewarding.

Human writes is a non-political group and while many of our members profess a faith, we are not a religious organization. We have a team of experienced coordinators, who provide support and guidance to members from the time of the initial letters being written and throughout the friendship and correspondence. We also have a team of trained counselors, who are available for additional help at times when it could be needed, such as when facing an execution, etc.

We hope you have enjoyed reading this book written by Sr. Joy Elder, who is a long-standing member of our organization. Further details can be obtained from:

Sue Lusk
Texas Coordinator, Human Writes
Uckfield, East Sussex, TN22 1UB
England
website: www.humanwrites.org